The
Genuine American
Cookie & Muffin
Book

☆ *This is it, the*
☆ *ultimate*
American
☆ *cookie and*
muffin book
☆ *for the British*
home baker.
☆ *Easy to follow*
recipes for kids
☆ *of all ages!*

☆

☆

Peter Shaffer

The Genuine American Cookie & Muffin Book

Published by Willow Publishing
P.O. Box 162
Beverley, E. Yorkshire
HU17 0WZ
enquiry@willowpublishing.info
www.willowpublishing.info

Illustrations by Doug Gray

First Published in Great Britain 2002

British Library Cataloguing in Publication Data

Data available

ISBN 0-9542931-0-X

Printed in Great Britain by Joseph Ward Colourprint
Churwell Vale, Shaw Cross Business Park, Dewsbury,
West Yorkshire WF12 7RD

Contents

Acknowledgements

This seems like a good time to thank my mom for all of her love & support throughout my life. For instilling in me the "can do" spirit and passing on her love of cooking and baking. Don't worry I have already said it a thousand times. Mom's 84 and her memory isn't what it used to be, so this will be a nice reminder.

To my children, Michael & Maggie for their unconditional love and support (more like constant nagging) in getting this book completed! For always being there when I needed that little extra bit of upliftment and inspiration. A dad could not ask for better kids!

And to all those that have touched my life and helped me become the person that I am today. Especially the team that helped me put this book together; Doug Gray for his great illustrations, Nicky Young for her graphic design work, Martin Stephenson from Dayfield Graphics for his design flair and technical expertise (what a star!) and Mike Mudryk for believing in the project as much as me. And all my neighbours and friends that have eaten their way through more muffins and cookies than I care to think about!

Introduction

We moved from California to North Yorkshire in 1992, don't ask why, it is a long story. Anyway, I love living in England (yes, I am out of my mind!) especially North Yorkshire, it is such a beautiful area and the locals are great! After 10 years I am now finding that the words "pardon", "excuse me" , "say what" and "come again" have just about left my vocabulary! I take great pride in saying that I can now speak fluent English, Yorkshire that is! Hey, you would think I was a local if I didn't have my American accent!

So why a cookie and muffin book? I have always loved baking and cooking, I had my formal training while in the US Navy at their Culinary School. And yes, I can make Navy Beans! We did have a restaurant in the North Yorkshire area for a few years and the cookies and muffins were very popular items. Customers were always asking for the recipes and on the odd occasion I would give them out. However, it was always in the back of my mind to put together a cookie and muffin book.

The other more compelling reason why I wanted to do the book was that there is little or no choice of cookie & muffin books in merry ol' England. I mean there are loads of books with lots of fancy cakes and pies, but when you have kids that have friends (*and I mean a lot of friends*) you need to be able to whip up sweet treats in a short time span with as little effort as possible. Whenever there are fresh baked cookies and muffins in our house they usually don't see the light of the second day! Hey, it's like "Day of The Locust", have you ever noticed how relentless kids are when it comes to eating! Especially sweets. Cookie monsters come to mind!

Anyone who has travelled to America knows that Americans love their cookies and muffins. You can tell by their size. . . not the muffins or cookies. . . the people! Anyway, with so many Brits vacationing in America every year, it is no wonder that we now see American muffins and cookies in local bake shops and supermarkets throughout the UK. Unfortunately, they do not offer much of a choice and that is what this book is about . . . choice. Giving you the choice of making your own absolutely fabulous cookies and muffins or settling for whatever is on offer at the local bake shop or supermarket.

I believe that if you have the brain power and manual dexterity to make beans on toast, you can certainly follow my fun and simple recipes. You will be amazed how easy it is to make up a batch of muffins or cookies, as a matter of fact, most of the recipes are safe for children to do with a bit of supervision. My kids love to bake and yours will too!

Kids do love to bake, and it is a wonderful way to get some quality time with them. If your kids are like mine, they are constantly glued in front of the tv or playing their computer games. But, as soon as I mention cookies and muffins they are more than happy to help out. Hey, they're not stupid, they know that in less than an hour they will be eating the end result of their effort! And what a great way to have some fun with them, no matter what their ages!

What you have before you is a collection of some of my favourite recipes all adopted for the British home baker. You can forget about American measures, a cup of this, a cup of that, what a carry on. You will be glad to see that all measures are by weight and fluid ounces. Oh, and to keep our friends in Brussels happy there are metric equivalents. And don't worry about the ingredients, all the ingredients in the recipes are readily available at your local scoop shop or supermarket. Happy baking!

Peter

we hold these truths to be self evident . . .
"a biscuit is a cookie. . .
and a fairy cake is a muffin"
and they should only be
served with coffee!

This is one of the first American flags. It had thirteen stars representing the thirteen original states.

The Story

Why do Americans call a biscuit a cookie and a fairy cake a muffin?

Believe it or not, according to legend it all has to do with the American Revolution! But before we answer that question of such great importance, I just want to say that I am amazed how little the Brits know about this period of American history. If nothing else, you should remember it as the only war where we showed up on time! Ok, ok, we were on the wrong side and you did have to come to us, but at least you didn't have to wait for us, we were on the shores when you landed! Come on, give us some credit.

Anyway, to get a clearer picture we have to go way back in time (*over two hundred years!*) around the early 1770's. Just a few years before the colonists declared their independence. I know, I know, you fought the Vikings and the Romans ruled the roost long before we were even a twinkle in your eyes! But hey, we are proud of our history, even if it only seems like a long weekend to you!

It is important to understand the mood of the colonists, who were not happy campers. The colonists were very independent minded men and women who risked everything, even their lives to settle a new world. As the colonies grew and prospered, the colonists became more and more resentful of the iron fist rule of King George III and the British Parliament. For a number of years the colonists had felt used and abused by the King and the Parliament, tensions were high.

Having said that, the British Parliament was not happy with the way things were going either. They felt that they were not getting enough income (*taxes*) from the colonies. (*Does that have a familiar ring?*) All through the 1760's & 1770's colonists objected to the various tax schemes that the Tory led Parliament was trying to impose on them. (*Amazing how history repeats itself!*)

Finally the colonists had had enough, on December 16, 1773 over 50 men dressed up as Indians and boarded British merchant ships anchored in the Boston harbour and threw 342 chests of tea overboard. The following day all of Boston was buzzing with stories of the "Tea Party", the mood was buoyant.

Everyone was having a good laugh about it, as the word spread through the colonies it became known as the "Boston Tea Party". The Boston Tea Party galvanised the colonists and for the first time they started to feel truly united in their quest for freedom and liberty.

A few days later, Abigail (*Abby*) Adams, the wife of John Adams (*one of the leaders of the Boston Tea Party*) was having afternoon tea with several other wives. They were all in a festive mood with Christmas and the New Year fast approaching. Since there was now an acute shortage of tea, all the ladies were having coffee! Everyone was still talking about the Tea Party and how brave and daring all their men were. Abby was feeling that the ladies needed to do something just as brave and daring. The ladies needed to do something for the Christmas season and the upcoming New Year, a new year with new beginnings. Something that would strike at the heart and soul of the British Empire, shake it to its very foundations.

As the ladies were sitting there talking, one of them said "if we are not having the King's tea, why should we still have his biscuits and fairy cakes!" Abby immediately shouted, "That's it, that's it, we won't have biscuits or fairy cakes!" But then Mrs Webster said "I like biscuits and fairy cakes, I just love my sweets, isn't there something else we can get rid of, how about imperial ounces?"

Abby immediately replied "no, no you silly woman, we will still have them to eat, we shall have our own". Just then Abby's neighbour Heidi came through the kitchen door with a platter full of biscuits and fairy cakes. She had overheard most of the conversation while she was in the kitchen. Heidi was Dutch and she went on to tell the ladies that in Holland they call biscuits "koekje's" which means "little cakes".

Abby repeated the word several times, how do you spell it Heidi, "k-o-e-k-j-e". The ladies all had a go at trying to pronounce it properly and decided it was too difficult.

Abby went over to her desk and got out her quill and paper, she wrote down the word and sat and stared at it for a few moments. She liked the name, but knew it had to be easier to pronounce and a word that would be identified as coming from the colonies. It came to her all at once, "I will drop the "k" and make it a "c", I will drop the "e" and make it an "o" and I will drop the "j" and make it an "i" and what does it spell. . . . "c-o-o-k-i-e"! Yes that's it" exclaimed Abby, she wrote it out in big bold letters and spun around in her chair and showed it to the rest of the ladies. They all read it aloud at the same time and shouted "COOKIES, that's it!" With that they jumped to their feet and started hugging each other.

The joy faded quickly when Mrs Webster said "what about the fairy cakes, what shall we call them?" Heidi responded by saying "when we were children, we called them 'little muffs'." My mother would always tell us to put the "muffs in", meaning to put the cakes in the oven. We called them "muffs" because they would keep our hands warm when they came out of the oven, laughing with the fond childhood memory, she said that is why my mother always said "put the muffs in."

Abby could not believe what she was hearing, she ran to Heidi and gave her a big hug and said "that's it, you have done it again", Heidi did not understand, and wanted to know "what have I done?" Abby exclaimed, "We are having COOKIES and MUFFINS." The ladies all shouted, "MUFFINS", yes, they knew that they were on to a winner. With that there were more hugs, and this time there were even a few high fives! *(The ladies would never do a high five in public, but in private they thought it was a bit naughty and daring, they were still English oriented!).* With that Abby exclaimed that American cookies and muffins would be bigger and better than the Kings biscuits and fairy cakes! *(Why do Americans always think that everything they do is bigger and better than everyone else. . . Hey, because it is!)*

The ladies spent the rest of the afternoon coming up with some of their own recipes for cookies and muffins to be circulated throughout the colonies. The news of this latest act of defiance spread like wildfire, along with the new recipes. Throughout the colonies ladies were feeling liberated, not only have we dumped the Kings tea, but we have thrown out his biscuits and fairy cakes as well! For the first time, the ladies felt that they were part of the rebellion, they had made their stance and there was no turning back. What a great way to celebrate Christmas and the coming New Year!

Well, King George got news of the Boston Tea Party the end of January 1774, it was the Colonial Secretary Lord George Germain that broke the news to him. Needless to say the King went absolutely ballistic, shouting "They did what? They did what?" They threw your tea into the harbour sire," repeated Lord Germain. "This is an outrage, I will have their heads, they will pay dearly for this" shouted the King. Cringing and shaking a bit, Lord Germain said "I am afraid there is more sire." "What do you mean more? Go on man, explain yourself" responded the King.

Lord Germain took a deep breath and said "well sire apparently they have thrown out our biscuits and fairy cakes as well." The King stood and shouted "They what? They what? What do you mean? Explain yourself man!" "Well sire it all has to do with that Abigail Adams, you know sire, John Adams wife. Apparently she felt that the ladies should take a stance along with their men, you know after the Boston Tea Party. So they decided that if the men could get rid of the tea, the ladies could get rid of the biscuits and fairy cakes, after all sire they do go together and it does make sense that if they are not having tea, they might as well not have. . .'Shut up you idiot, this is an absolute outrage!", shouted the King.

By now the King was pacing the palace floor ranting and raving. "I will not tolerate this, they have gone too far, how dare they throw my tea into the Boston Harbour, how dare they give up our biscuits, how dare they give up our fairy cakes, have they gone mad? And what will they have instead of biscuits and fairy cakes?"

"Well sire, there was mention of coffee, cookies and muffins", responded Lord Germain. "Have they gone mad?" shouted the King. "Well sire, I think that they actually prefer coffee" responded Lord Germain. "Shut up you idiot, everyone knows that in the civilised world ladies and gentlemen drink tea and they have biscuits and fairy cakes with it, not COOKIES and MUFFINS." The King immediately dispatched Lord Germain to the British Parliament demanding that they take immediate action to punish these latest acts of rebellion.

The British Parliament was as outraged as the King over the Boston Tea Party. They were stunned at the thought of these colonial women acting so independent and how dare they, how dare they think that they can do away with one of the oldest traditions in England, tea with biscuits and fairy cakes.

The British Parliament agreed with their King that they must not tolerate this rebellious behaviour. On March 31, 1774, the King approved the first of parliamentary reprisals known as the "Intolerable Acts". *(Hey, these guys did not mess around; they were going to sort the colonists out in no time!)* In order to punish Boston for the Tea Party, the port was to be closed until the colonial authorities pay for the destroyed tea. This was bad news for Boston and the rest of the colonies. The colonies now had a population of over 2.5 million people and the ports were their lifelines. Boston was one of the busiest ports, with well over 50 merchant ships in the harbour at any one time.

Later measures included a ban on any public meetings without the Governor's approval; a requirement that British troops be housed in private dwellings wherever necessary. *(Having the soldiers in every home in Boston looked good on paper, but it wasn't practical. I mean if someone wants to make cookies and muffins you just can not keep an eye on them for 24 hours a day, can you?).*

The colonists were outraged with the "Intolerable Acts", how dare the King try to stop them from making cookies and muffins in their own homes. That was it. On September 5, 1774 the First Continental Congress met in Philadelphia for nearly two months and did they go through some coffee, cookies and muffins! At the end of their meeting they issued a declaration of ten "rights," including "life, liberty and property", and "a right to peaceably assemble" and just to really wind the King up, they included. . ."We hold these truths to be self evident a biscuit is a cookie and a fairy cake is a muffin and they should only be served with coffee" they petitioned the King.

Well, as the old saying goes. . ."the rest is history". King George went absolutely mad when he received the petition. He was ok with the right to life and liberty and he did not mind too much if they assembled peacefully, but this thing with the cookies and muffins was more than he could take. What really upset him was that no one even offered him one!

So the British troops were sent into action and there were many confrontations over the next 18 months. Then on July 4, 1776, the First Continental Congress approved the Declaration of Independence without one dissenting colony. It was signed by Congress President John Hancock and ordered "proclaimed in each of the United States."

July 4, 1776 marked the official beginning of the American Revolution; the colonists knew that once they declared their independence there would be no turning back. Every man, woman and child would have to stand tall and be counted, for their fight was right and just. They were determined to win the right to . . . . Call a biscuit a cookie and a fairy cake a muffin!

Cookies

MAKING COOKIES ~ THE BASICS

The great thing about making cookies is that they are fun and easy to do. My attitude is if you can crack an egg, open a bag of flour, then you can certainly throw together some great cookies! And they don't necessarily require expensive ingredients or special utensils. However, baking cookies will be easier and more fun if you are equipped with a few basic items.

Here's what you will need ~ a couple of baking sheets (aluminium or non-stick will do); and a standard square baking tin. The most frequently used sizes are the 8-inch square and 9-inch square baking tins. If you are new to baking and do not have these tins, DON'T PANIC, go borrow them from your friends, neighbours or relatives!

If they don't have what you need, then go out and treat yourself. An electric mixer or food processor would cut down on the preparation time however, you can cream your butter mixture and mix your cookie dough by hand. You will also need mixing bowls, measuring spoons, a measuring cup, scale, spatula (rubber or metal), and wire whisk.

Making cookies is not hard it just takes a little organization. Before starting, roll up your sleeves, put on your apron and wash your hands, then read your recipe and assemble all the ingredients and equipment.

Grease the tins only if the recipe calls for it. If you are required to grease a tin, use baking margarine, vegetable shortening or a non-stick vegetable spray (not lard - YUK! Sorry I'm a vegetarian).

Know your oven. Keep in mind that the top position in the oven will be hotter than the bottom position that is why it is best to use the middle position of the oven when baking.

You may want to test your oven with an oven thermometer; if the settings don't reflect the oven temperature, adjust the temperature accordingly. Check your cookies for doneness towards the end of the low range of suggested baking time, and then keep an eye on them until they are ready. Cookies can quickly over-bake, so if you are like me and have short-term memory dysfunction, you may want to use a timer with a loud bell!

Common sense should always prevail in the kitchen, however, if you are new to baking here's a few tips:

★ Never lick your fingers, utensils or the bowl when someone is watching!

★ If someone is watching or catches you, immediately invite them to join in! Only kidding . . . because the dough contains raw eggs it is a good idea not to lick your fingers, the spoon or the bowl as there is a slim chance of becoming ill from the salmonella bacteria.

★ Use proper measuring spoons; do not use household teaspoons and tablespoons for measuring. All measures should be level to the top of the spoon, not rounded.

★ Always use the same amount of dough for each cookie. This will ensure uniform baking.

★ Always use a cool baking sheet. A hot baking sheet causes dough to soften and spread to quickly. It is best to have three baking sheets! Tell you why later.

★ Using the centre position of the oven, bake one sheet of cookies at a time. Remember check cookies for doneness at the low range of the baking time. The cookies should be firmly set and slightly browned. When you touch them lightly with your finger no imprint should remain. One minute or two can make the difference between a perfect cookie and an over baked one!

★ Unless the recipe states otherwise, allow the cookies to stand for 1 or 2 minutes to firm up before removing from the baking sheet. Remove with a spatula that is at least as wide as the cookie and place on a wire rack or cool surface. Cool completely before eating and/or storing.

★ If you want to bake ahead cookies are freezer friendly, especially bar cookies. Store them in containers with tight fitting lids for up six months. Thaw at room temperature.

Let's have a quick look at equipment and ingredients;

★ **Oven.** All baking times & temperatures are for a conventional or gas oven. For a fan-assisted oven, the temperature should be reduced approximately 20°C or one Gas Mark, also the baking time should be shortened by a few minutes. Again, as oven temperatures can vary it is best to check your oven with an oven thermometer to ensure that the oven settings match the temperatures.

★ **Electric Mixer.** Electric mixers are great for creaming the butter, sugar and eggs. I do find it a lot easier using a large spoon to mix in the dry ingredients instead of the electric mixer, your call!

★**Food Processor.** I find using the food processor to be the quickest and easiest way of making cookie dough. Using the dough blade start off by creaming your butter, sugar and eggs, then simply add in the dry ingredients and pulse until all ingredients are combined. Do not over mix!

★ **Baking Sheets.** It is best to have at least three, bake with one, prepare the second and cool the third! Shiny aluminium cookie sheets are the best. The shiny metal reflects heat so the cookies will not bake as quickly and there is less chance of over-baking. Dark non-reflective surface sheets bake faster. You must watch your baking times more closely when using non-reflective sheets.

★ **Flour.** All the recipes were tested with plain flour (store brand, works great and its inexpensive) measured straight from the package (sorry I don't sift). Flour absorption rates can vary as much as 20%, however, these variations will not make an appreciable difference in the finished product. You should not use self raising flour when making cookies. As you will see a few of the recipes call for wholemeal plain flour. If you do not have any or you are not keen on wholemeal flour substitute plain flour.

★ **Butter.** Well, I prefer the flavour of butter, which is why the majority of recipes in this book call for it. Yes of course you can use margarine; my preference here is baking margarine. I do not recommend substituting low-fat spreads. They contain a higher proportion of water and air, which means that the quality of the finished product will be less predictable.

★ **Sugar.** Sugar adds sweetness, tenderness and moistness to recipes while it aids in browning. In general my preference is soft Demerara sugar it enhances the flavour without overpowering the other ingredients. White granulated sugar is a must for the fruit cookies as their flavour is so delicate.

★ **Eggs.** The recipes in this book have been tested using large eggs. If you use a different size the recipe results may differ. Having said that, I have had equal success with medium eggs.

★ **Flavouring.** Now I know this will upset the connoisseurs out there but most of the time I do use flavouring instead of natural essence. Why, well until just recently natural essence was not widely available so I have gotten in the habit of using the flavouring. Besides, the way my kids and their friends go through the cookies I honestly do not think they would know or appreciate the difference! Having said that I do use natural essence when I am baking for big kids (adults!) Hey, I want to make a good impression.

★ **Vegetable oil.** You can not substitute vegetable oil for butter.

★ **Baking powder and Bicarbonate of Soda.** Both of these are used as leaveners for many of the cookie recipes. Baking soda is used to neutralize acidic ingredients. Baking powder is not interchangeable with bicarbonate of soda.

★ **When doubling a recipe,** cut back on seasonings such as salt, cinnamon, etc. If a single recipe calls for 1 teaspoon seasoning, for doubling only use 1½ teaspoons.

In America cookies are categorised by the way that they are formed. There are several different categories of cookies, drop; bar; molded; refrigerator; rolled and pressed. My favourites are drop and bar cookies, the variations are endless, these are the types that are featured in this book.

Drop Cookies - The dough is dropped by spoonfuls onto a baking sheet. I find that using a soup spoon or a household tablespoon and pushing the dough off with my index finger is the easiest way for me. When baked, your drop cookies should be slightly mounded and fairly uniform in shape with a very light brown exterior.

Bar Cookies - Basically all of your cookie dough is spread into a square or rectangular pan, and baked! It is then cut into bars, squares or triangles, whatever your preference.

With bar cookies it is important to use the size pan specified in the recipe. If you do not have the proper size pan remember that you will need to adjust your baking times. If you do not adjust your baking times, bar cookies made in a larger pan will be dry and over-baked; in a smaller pan, under-baked and very chewy! Remember, do not cut your bar cookies until they are completely cool, unless the recipe states otherwise, or if you just can't wait because they smell and look sooo good!

Come on; let's go check out the recipes. . . . . .

Apricot - Almond Squares

Preheat oven to Gas Mark 4 / 180°C / 350°F

Pastry

5oz / 140g	plain flour
4oz / 115g	butter, soft
2oz / 60g	granulated sugar

Filling

7oz / 200g	dried apricots
8fl oz / 240ml	water
2oz / 60g	plain flour
½ teaspoon / 2.5ml	baking powder
¼ teaspoon / 1.2ml	salt
7oz / 200g	granulated sugar
2	large eggs
1 teaspoon / 5ml	vanilla flavouring or natural essence
½ teaspoon / 2.5ml	almond flavouring or natural essence
1oz / 25g	Sliced Almonds
	Icing sugar

Place apricots in a small saucepan; cover with water. Bring to a boil over medium-high heat. Simmer until tender (8 to 10 minutes). Drain, when cool cut into thin slivers. Set aside.

Pastry: While the apricots simmer; in a medium bowl, cream butter and sugar, gradually add flour mix until smooth. Press evenly into the bottom of an ungreased 9x9x2inch square baking tin. I like using my fingers for this job! Don't forget about your apricots.

Bake pastry on the centre rack of oven for 20 minutes.

Filling: While pastry is baking, in a small bowl combine plain flour, baking powder and salt. Set aside. In a medium bowl, beat eggs until thick and creamy, gradually add sugar. Blend in flour mixture, vanilla and almond essence. Stir in apricots.

Remove pastry from the oven and spread apricot mixture evenly over hot pastry, spinkle with sliced almonds and return to centre rack of oven for another 25 minutes. DO NOT OVERBAKE.

Cool on a wire rack to room temperature. Top with icing sugar and cut into snack size 2 inch squares or for a rich delicious dessert, cut into larger pieces and serve with cream or a dollop of whipped cream - Mmmmmm.

☆
☆
☆
☆
☆
☆
☆
☆
☆

Hey don't worry these are just square cookies! So why call them "bar" cookies if they are square? Well, if I had to venture a guess they were probably originally cut into bar or rectangular shape and the name just stuck! Unless someone else has a better answer!?

Apricot Raisin Pecan Cookies

Preheat oven to Gas Mark 4 / 180°C / 350°F
This recipe will yield approximately 30 cookies.

Place apricots, raisins and 8fl oz (240ml) water in a medium sauce pan. Cover and bring to a boil, simmer for 3-4 minutes. Remove from heat, allow to cool. DO NOT DRAIN.

7oz / 200g	dried apricots, finely chopped
5oz / 140g	seedless raisins

In a medium bowl add and combine with a fork or wire whisk ~

1lb 1oz / 490g	plain flour
1 teaspoon / 5ml	bicarbonate of soda
1 teaspoon / 5ml	baking powder
½ teaspoon / 2.5ml	ground cinnamon
½ teaspoon / 2.5ml	ground nutmeg
1 teaspoon / 5ml	salt
3½ oz / 100g	pecans, chopped

In a large bowl cream butter, sugar, and flavouring. Scrape down the sides of the bowl, add eggs, blend well, now add apricots & raisins with water blend well ~

9oz / 250g	soft Demerara sugar
8oz / 225g	butter, softened
2	large eggs
1 teaspoon / 5ml	vanilla flavouring/natural essence

Gradually fold dry ingredients into butter mixture. Because the cookie dough is very stiff, I find it easier to mix with a large spoon - wood, plastic or metal your choice. Just mix long enough to combine the ingredients, do not over-mix.

Using a tablespoon drop cookie dough by rounded portions 1½ to 2 inch (3-5cm) in size onto baking sheet 2 to 3 inches (5-8cm) apart. Bake for approximately 12 to 15 minutes for a soft centre cookie slightly browned. Allow cookies to stand for one or two minutes to firm up before removing from the baking sheet. Transfer cookies to a wire rack or cool surface.

What a delightful combination of ingredients, I hate to say it, but these go great with a cuppa!

Banana, Nut & Rolled Oat Cookies

Preheat oven to Gas Mark 4 / 180°C / 350°F
This recipe will yield 18 to 24 cookies.

In a medium bowl add and combine with a fork or wire whisk ~

10oz / 280g	plain flour
1 teaspoon / 5ml	bicarbonate of soda
1 teaspoon / 5ml	baking powder
1 teaspoon / 5ml	salt
3oz / 85g	rolled oats (do not use instant oats!)
2oz / 60g	nuts, chopped – pecans or walnuts

In a large bowl cream butter, sugar, and flavouring. Scrape down the sides of the bowl, add eggs, lemon juice and bananas, blend well ~

6oz / 175g	soft Demerara sugar
5oz / 150g	butter, softened
2	large eggs
1 teaspoon / 5ml	vanilla flavouring/natural essence
1 teaspoon / 5ml	lemon juice
1 ½	bananas, medium ~ mashed

Gradually fold dry ingredients into butter mixture. Because the cookie dough is very stiff, I find it easier to mix with a large spoon - wood, plastic or metal your choice. Just mix long enough to combine the ingredients, do not over-mix.

Using a tablespoon drop cookie dough by rounded portions 1 ½ to 2 inch (3-5cm) in size onto baking sheet 2 to 3 inches (5-8cm) apart. Bake for approximately 15 to 18 minutes for a soft centre cookie, slightly browned. Allow cookies to stand for one or two minutes to firm up before removing from the baking sheet. Transfer cookies to a wire rack or cool surface.

TIP: DO NOT mash the bananas with your FEET! They are really hard to get off the floor!

This cookie is not chewy, more like a small cake. It is very light and not very filling, which means that you can eat a lot of them at one sitting!

Black Cherry Hazelnut Cookies

Preheat oven to Gas Mark 3 / 170°C / 325°F
This recipe will yield 18 to 24 cookies.

In a medium bowl add and combine with a fork or wire whisk

10oz / 280g	plain flour
3 ½ oz / 100g	hazelnuts, chopped

In a large bowl cream butter, sugar, and flavouring. Scrape down the sides of the bowl, add egg, blend well ~

8oz / 225g	butter, softened
5oz / 150g	icing sugar
1 teaspoon / 5ml	vanilla flavouring/natural essence
1	large egg

FILLING: Black Cherry Jam 4oz /115g

Gradually fold dry ingredients into butter mixture. Because the cookie dough is very stiff, I find it easier to mix with a large spoon - wood, plastic or metal your choice. Just mix long enough to combine the ingredients, do not over-mix.

Using a tablespoon drop cookie dough by rounded portions 1 to 1 ½ inch (3-4.5cm) in size onto baking sheet 2 to 3 inches (5-8cm) apart. With spoon or thumb, make an imprint in the centre of each cookie. Fill each with about ½ teaspoon jam.

Bake for approximately 15 to 20 minutes for a soft centre cookie slightly browned. Allow cookies to stand for one or two minutes to firm up before removing from the baking sheet. Transfer cookies to a wire rack or cool surface.

VARIATION: Grandma says that these would be great for Christmas treats if you used prepared mincemeat or jellied cranberries instead of jam! Sounds good to me.

This really is a delightful combination, but if you are not keen on black cherries then use your favourite jam!

TIP: A 340g jar of jam is enough for two batches of cookies!

Cashew Cookies

Preheat oven to Gas Mark 5 / 190°C / 375°F
This recipe will yield 18 to 24 cookies.

In a medium bowl add and combine with a fork or wire whisk

10oz / 280g	plain flour
1 teaspoon / 5ml	baking powder
1 teaspoon / 5ml	bicarbonate soda
5oz / 150g	salted cashews, coarsely chopped

In a large bowl cream butter, sugar, and flavouring. Scrape down the sides of the bowl, add soured cream & egg, blend well ~

4oz / 115g	butter, softened
6oz / 175g	soft Demerara sugar
1 teaspoon / 5ml	vanilla flavouring/natural essence
1	large egg
4 Tablespoons / 60ml	soured cream

TOPPING: Icing sugar

Gradually fold dry ingredients into butter mixture. Because the cookie dough is very stiff, I find it easier to mix with a large spoon - wood, plastic or metal your choice. Just mix long enough to combine the ingredients, do not over-mix.

Using a tablespoon drop cookie dough by rounded portions 1 ½ to 2 inch (3-5cm) in size onto baking sheet 2 to 3 inches (5-8cm) apart. Bake for approximately 8 to 10 minutes for a soft centre cookie slightly browned. Allow cookies to stand for one or two minutes to firm up before removing from the baking sheet. Transfer cookies to a wire rack or cool surface. Dust with icing sugar.

Let's face it when we are at a party and no one is looking, this is the nut that we all pick out of the cocktail mixes!

Chocolate Chip Walnut Bars

Heads up! You will need three 100g packs of plain chocolate chips for this recipe!

Preheat oven to Gas Mark 5 - 190°C - 375°F
Grease a 9x9x2inch square baking tin

In a medium bowl add and combine with a fork or wire whisk ~

6oz / 175g	plain flour
½ teaspoon / 2.5ml	bicarbonate of soda
½ teaspoon / 2.5ml	salt
7oz / 200g	plain chocolate chips (2 – 100g packs!)
4oz / 115g	walnuts, chopped

In another bowl cream butter, sugar, and flavouring. Scrape down the sides of the bowl, add egg, blend well

4oz / 115g	butter, soft
6oz / 175g	soft Demerara sugar
1 teaspoon / 5ml	vanilla flavouring or natural essence
1	large eggs

Gradually fold dry ingredients into butter mixture. Because the cookie dough is very stiff, I find it easier to mix with a large spoon - wood, plastic or metal your choice. Just mix long enough to combine the ingredients, do not over-mix. Spread batter into greased pan. Smooth surface with a spatula or the back of your spoon.

Bake on the centre rack of the oven for 20 to 25 minutes. The walnut bars are done when the batter is set and you touch them lightly and there is no indentation. DO NOT OVERBAKE! Remove from oven and immediately sprinkle one 3½ oz / 100g packet of chocolate chips over top. When chips become soft, spread evenly. Cool on wire rack to room temperature. When cool, chill 5 -10 minutes to set chocolate. Cut into 2 inch (5cm) squares or bars and enjoy!

Hey, anyway you cut this one . . . bars, squares, triangles or even circles they are going to taste great!

Chocolate Peanut Butter Crunch

This is it Grandma's all time favourite!

This is a mix and chill dish, so you will not need your oven!
Butter a 9x9x2inch baking tin

In a medium bowl add and combine with a large spoon ~

8oz / 225g	cornflake cereal
7oz / 200g	chocolate chips, plain
4oz / 115g	peanuts, salted

In a medium size heavy saucepan heat peanut butter, honey and sugar over a medium - low heat. Stir and heat until smooth. DO NOT SCORCH OR BURN!

9oz / 250g	Peanut Butter (smooth)
11oz / 300g	Honey, clear
3oz / 85g	soft Demerara sugar

Carefully add peanut butter mixture to cornflake mixture. Mix until well combined. The chocolate chips will melt from the heat of the peanut butter mixture.

Spread mixture into a prepared baking tin. Use the back of the mixing spoon (a large one) to press the mixture into the tin so that you have a nice flat surface. This will take some effort, but it is worth it!

The most common question at this point is. . . . Mmmm, can I eat them now?! Sorry, NO, chill in the refrigerator for 1 to 2 hours, and then cut into approximately 18 bars. These crunchy bars are very addictive, it is difficult to eat just one! Save yourself a trip to the kitchen and take two at a time!

Variation: Instead of honey use the same amount of golden syrup.

TIP: Do not worry about trying to weigh the honey or golden syrup, use ¾ of a 454g tin or jar, you can be a little over or under.

Chocolate-Chocolate Chip Cookies
Attention Chocoholics ~ this one is for you!

Preheat oven to Gas Mark 3 / 170°C / 325°F
This recipe will yield 18 to 24 cookies.

In a medium bowl add and combine with a fork or wire whisk ~

12oz / 350g *8oz*	plain flour
½ teaspoon / 2.5ml *¼*	bicarbonate of soda
½ teaspoon / 2.5ml *¼*	salt
4oz / 115g *½*	unsweetened cocoa powder
11oz / 300g *8oz*	plain chocolate chips (3 - 100g packs!)

In a large bowl cream butter, sugar, and vanilla. Scrape down the sides of the bowl, add eggs, blend well ~

8oz / 225g *5½*	dark brown sugar
4oz / 115g *1½*	soft Demerara sugar
8oz / 225g *5½*	butter, softened
3 *2*	large eggs
2 teaspoons / 10ml *1*	vanilla flavouring/natural essence

Gradually fold dry ingredients into butter mixture. Because the cookie dough is very stiff, I find it easier to mix with a large spoon - wood, plastic or metal your choice. Just mix long enough to combine the ingredients, do not over-mix.

Using a tablespoon drop cookie dough by rounded portions 1½ to 2 inch (3-5cm) in size onto baking sheet 2 to 3 inches (5-8cm) apart. Bake for approximately 18 to 20 minutes for a soft centre cookie. Transfer cookies to a wire rack or cool surface.

Variation: How about **Triple Chocolate Chip Cookies**? Substitute 150g white chocolate bar coarse chopped for 200g plain chocolate chips.

This is the most popular cookie to bake for fund raisers! When the kids were in primary school I would always bake a couple of dozen for their table to sell on Red Nose Day. They always sold out first, I told them to raise the price, you know supply and demand, but they wouldn't do it!

☆ ☆ ☆ ☆ ☆ ☆ ☆ ☆ ☆

Classic Chocolate Chip Cookies

Chocolate chip cookies are one of America's all time favourites!

Preheat oven to Gas Mark 3 / 170°C / 325°F
This recipe will yield approximately 30 cookies.

In a medium bowl add and combine with a fork or wire whisk ~

12oz / 360g	plain flour
½ teaspoon / 2.5ml	bicarbonate of soda
½ teaspoon / 2.5ml	salt
11oz / 300g	plain chocolate chips (3 – 100g packs!)

In a large bowl cream butter, sugar, and flavouring. Scrape down the sides of the bowl, add eggs blend well ~

8oz / 225g	dark brown sugar
4oz / 115g	soft Demerara sugar
8oz / 225g	butter, softened
2	large eggs
2 teaspoons / 10ml	vanilla flavouring/natural essence

Gradually fold dry ingredients into butter mixture. Because the cookie dough is very stiff, I find it easier to mix with a large spoon - wood, plastic or metal your choice. Just mix long enough to combine the ingredients, do not over-mix.

Using a tablespoon drop cookie dough by rounded portions 1 ½ to 2 inch (3-5cm) in size onto baking sheet 2 to 3 inches (5-8cm) apart. Bake for approximately 18 to 20 minutes for a soft centre cookie, slightly browned. Transfer cookies to a wire rack or cool surface.

Here is another one that is great for fundraisers or parties. Simple and easy, always popular. Hey, if you want to be the talk of the party just bring some of these babies along!

Deluxe Superfudge Brownies

Preheat oven to Gas Mark 4 / 180°C / 350°F
Grease an 9x9x2inch square baking tin

In a large bowl add and combine with a fork or wire whisk

6oz / 175g	plain flour
4oz / 115g	unsweetened cocoa powder
3oz / 85g	walnuts, chopped
3 ½ oz / 100g	plain chocolate chips

In a medium bowl cream butter, sugar, and flavouring. Scrape down the sides of the bowl, add eggs blend well ~

9oz / 250g	butter, soft
4oz / 115g	soft Demerara sugar
6oz / 175g	dark brown sugar
4	large eggs
1 Tablespoon / 15ml	vanilla flavouring / natural essence

Gradually fold dry ingredients into butter mixture. Because the cookie dough is very stiff, I find it easier to mix with a large spoon - wood, plastic or metal your choice. Just mix long enough to combine the ingredients, do not over-mix. Spoon batter into prepared tin. Smooth surface with a spatula or the back of your spoon.

Bake on the centre rack of the oven for approximately 35 to 40 minutes. The brownies are done when a toothpick inserted about 2 inches (5cm) from the side comes out clean. DO NOT OVERBAKE!

Cool on wire rack to room temperature, usually about an hour. Cut into 2 inch squares and enjoy! Mmmmmm. . . .

These brownies have a very moist texture making them deliciously chewy, a mouth watering treat!.

Easy Traditional Brownies
The name says it all, not only are they e-a-s-y, but they are delicious!

Preheat oven to Gas Mark 4 / 180°C / 350°F
Grease an 9x9x2inch square baking tin

In a medium bowl add and combine with a fork or wire whisk ~

5oz / 140g	plain flour
2oz / 60g	unsweetened cocoa powder
3oz / 85g	walnuts, chopped
3½ oz / 100g	plain chocolate chips (optional)

In another bowl cream butter, sugar, and flavouring. Scrape down the sides of the bowl, add eggs blend well ~

6oz / 175g	butter
10oz /275g	soft Demerara sugar
3	large eggs
2 teaspoons / 10ml	vanilla flavouring or natural essence

I told you this is an E A S Y recipe!   Gradually fold dry ingredients into butter mixture. Because the cookie dough is very stiff, I find it easier to mix with a large spoon - wood, plastic or metal your choice. Just mix long enough to combine the ingredients, do not over-mix. Spoon batter into tin, smooth with the back of spoon or a spatula.

Bake on the centre rack of the oven for 30 to 35 minutes. Your brownies are done when the batter is set and a toothpick inserted in the centre comes out clean. DO NOT OVERBAKE! Cool on wire rack to room temperature, usually about an hour. Cut into 2-inch (5cm) squares and enjoy!

Tip: Cocoa powder is very fine. Take care when adding it to the dry ingredients otherwise it will be all over your work top!

Lemon Poppy Seed Cookies

Preheat oven to Gas Mark 3 / 170°C / 325°F
This recipe will yeild approximately 24 cookies.

In a medium bowl add and combine with a fork or wire whisk ~

10oz / 280g	plain flour
½ teaspoon / 2.5ml	bicarbonate of soda
1 teaspoon / 5ml	ground coriander
2 Tablespoons / 30ml	poppy seeds

In a large bowl cream butter, sugar, and flavouring. Scrape down the sides of the bowl, add eggs and lemon zest, blend well ~

6oz / 175g	granulated sugar
6oz / 175g	butter, softened
2	large eggs
1	yolk, large
1 teaspoon	lemon flavouring/natural essence
2	lemons, grated rind only

Gradually fold dry ingredients into butter mixture. Because the cookie dough is very stiff, I find it easier to mix with a large spoon - wood, plastic or metal your choice. Just mix long enough to combine the ingredients, do not over-mix.

Using a tablespoon drop cookie dough by rounded portions 1 ½ to 2 inch (3-5cm) in size onto baking sheet 2 to 3 inches (5-8cm) apart. Bake for approximately 20 to 25 minutes for a soft centre cookie, slightly browned. Transfer cookies to a wire rack or cool surface.

These will make your lips pucker up!

If you like these you should try the Tangy Lemon Squares or how about the Lemon Poppy Seed Muffins!

Mocha Squares
coffee and chocolate.... Mmmmmm!

Preheat oven to Gas Mark 4 / 180°C / 350°F
Grease a 9x9x2inch square baking tin

In a medium bowl add and combine with a fork or wire whisk

10oz / 280g	plain flour
2 teaspoons / 10ml	baking powder
7oz / 200g	plain chocolate chips
4oz / 115g	pecans, chopped
½ teaspoon / 2.5ml	salt

In a cup combine instant coffee and boiling water. In large bowl cream butter, sugar, and flavouring. Scrape down the sides of the bowl, add eggs and coffee, blend well ~

4oz / 115g	butter, soft
9oz / 250g	soft Demerara sugar
2	large eggs
2 Tablespoons / 30ml	instant coffee
1 Tablespoon / 15ml	boiling water
1 teaspoon / 5ml	vanilla flavouring / natural essence

Gradually fold dry ingredients into butter mixture. Because the cookie dough is very stiff, I find it easier to mix with a large spoon - wood, plastic or metal your choice. Just mix long enough to combine the ingredients, do not over-mix. Spread batter into greased pan. Smooth surface with a spatula or the back of your spoon.

Bake on the centre position of the oven for 25 to 30 minutes, Your squares are done when the batter is set and a toothpick inserted in the centre comes out clean. DO NOT OVERBAKE! Cool on wire rack to room temperature, usually about an hour. Cut into 2-inch (5cm) squares and enjoy!

Variation: How about adding 2oz / 60g of chopped hazelnuts!

Oatmeal Raisin Cookies

Preheat oven to Gas Mark 4 / 180°C / 350°F
This recipe will yield approximately 30 cookies.

In a medium bowl add and combine with a fork or wire whisk ~

10oz / 280g	plain flour
1 teaspoon / 5ml	bicarbonate of soda
1 teaspoon / 5ml	salt
5oz / 150g	seedless raisins
1 teaspoon / 5ml	ground cinnamon
9oz / 250g	rolled oats (do not use instant oats!)

In a large bowl cream butter, sugar, and flavouring. Scrape down the sides of the bowl, add eggs, blend well ~

7oz / 200g	soft Demerara sugar
8oz / 225g	dark brown sugar
8oz / 225g	butter, softened
2	large eggs
1 teaspoon / 5ml	vanilla flavouring/natural essence

Gradually fold dry ingredients into butter mixture. Because the cookie dough is very stiff, I find it easier to mix with a large spoon - wood, plastic or metal your choice. Just mix long enough to combine the ingredients, do not over-mix.

Using a tablespoon drop cookie dough by rounded portions 1½ to 2 inch (3-5cm) in size onto baking sheet 2 to 3 inches (5-8cm) apart. Bake for approximately 15 to 18 minutes for a soft centre cookie, slightly browned. Allow cookies to stand for one or two minutes to firm up before removing from the baking sheet. Transfer cookies to a wire rack or cool surface.

Variations: Why not add plain chocolate chips or chopped walnuts. 5 to 6oz (140g to 175g) of either one or be daring and add a combination of both! Baking is all about experimenting and having a bit of fun!

I can remember baking these as a child . . . this one is my mom's all time favourite!

Orange Chocolate Chip Cookies

Preheat oven to Gas Mark 3 / 170°C / 325°F
This recipe will yield 18 to 24 cookies.

In a medium bowl add and combine with a fork or wire whisk ~

12oz / 350g	plain flour
7oz / 200g	plain chocolate chips
½ teaspoon / 2.5ml	bicarbonate of soda
½ teaspoon / 2.5ml	salt

In a large bowl cream butter, sugar, and flavouring. Scrape down the sides of the bowl, add eggs and orange zest blend well.

4oz / 115g	dark brown sugar
7oz / 200g	soft Demerara sugar
8oz / 225g	butter, softened
2	large eggs
1 teaspoon / 5ml	orange flavouring/natural essence
2	medium oranges, grated zest only

Gradually fold dry ingredients into butter mixture. Because the cookie dough is very stiff, I find it easier to mix with a large spoon - wood, plastic or metal your choice. Just mix long enough to combine the ingredients, do not over-mix.

Using a tablespoon drop cookie dough by rounded portions 1½ to 2 inch (3-5cm) in size onto baking sheet 2 to 3 inches (5-8cm) apart. Bake for approximately 18 to 20 minutes for a soft centre cookie, make sure they are slightly browned. Transfer cookies to a wire rack or cool surface.

Florida Specials!
Orange and
chocolate chips,
a taste to die for!

Peanut Butter Cookies
These are great with a glass of ice cold milk!

Preheat oven to Gas Mark 5 / 190°C / 375°F
This recipe will yield 18 to 24 cookies.

In a medium bowl add and combine with a fork or wire whisk

12oz / 350g	plain flour
2 teaspoons / 10ml	bicarbonate of soda
1 teaspoon / 5ml	baking powder
7oz / 200g	soft Demerara sugar
8oz / 225g	dark brown sugar

In a large bowl cream butter, peanut butter, sugar, and flavouring. Scrape down the sides of the bowl, add eggs, blend well ~

8oz / 225g	butter, soft
9oz / 250g	peanut butter, smooth
2	large eggs
1 teaspoon / 5ml	vanilla flavouring/natural essence

Gradually fold dry ingredients into butter mixture. Because the cookie dough is very stiff, I find it easier to mix with a large spoon - wood, plastic or metal your choice. Just mix long enough to combine the ingredients, do not over-mix.

Using a tablespoon drop cookie dough by rounded portions 1 ½ to 2 inch (3-5cm) in size onto baking sheet 2 to 3 inches (5-8cm) apart. Flatten with a fork in a crisscross pattern leaving dough about ½ inch (1.5cm) thick. Bake for approximately 8 to 10 minutes or until golden brown. Do not overbake! Transfer cookies to a wire rack or cool surface.

Variation: Try adding plain chocolate chips, just add two 100g packs to the dry ingredients. Peanut butter and chocolate . . . Mmmm!

TIP: Hey, why don't you gently press two or three salted peanuts onto tops of each cookie before baking. They really look nice when they come out of the oven, and taste good too!

Pecan Blondies

Preheat oven to Gas Mark 4 / 180°C / 350°F
Grease a 9x9x2 inch square baking tin

In a medium bowl add and combine with a fork or wire whisk ~

7oz / 200g	plain flour
½ teaspoon / 2.5ml	bicarbonate of soda
3½ oz/ 100g	plain chocolate chips (optional)
2oz / 60g	pecans, chopped

In a large bowl cream butter, sugar, and flavouring. Scrape down the sides of the bowl, add eggs, blend well ~

4oz / 115g	butter
6oz / 175g	soft Demerara sugar
2	large eggs
2 teaspoons / 10ml	vanilla flavouring or natural essence

Gradually fold dry ingredients into butter mixture. Because the cookie dough is very stiff, I find it easier to mix with a large spoon - wood, plastic or metal your choice. Just mix long enough to combine the ingredients, do not over-mix. Spread batter into greased tin. Smooth surface with a spatula or the back of your spoon.

Bake on the centre rack of the oven for 30 to 35 minutes. Your blondies are done when the batter is set and a toothpick inserted in the centre comes out clean. DO NOT OVERBAKE! Cool on wire rack to room temperature, usually about an hour. Cut into 2 inch (5cm) squares and enjoy!

Brownies without the cocoa, a scrumptious delight with a bit of cream!

Pecan Royales

Preheat oven to Gas Mark 3 / 170°C / 325°F
This recipe will yield approximately 30 cookies.

In a medium bowl add and combine with a fork or wire whisk ~

10oz / 280g	plain flour
2oz / 60g	rolled oats
7oz / 200g	plain chocolate chips
3½ oz / 100g	pecans, chopped
½ teaspoon / 2.5ml	bicarbonate of soda
½ teaspoon / 2.5ml	salt

In a large bowl cream butter, sugar, and flavouring. Scrape down the sides of the bowl, add eggs, blend well ~

6oz / 175g	dark brown sugar
5oz / 150g	soft Demerara sugar
8oz / 225g	butter, softened
2	large eggs
2 teaspoons / 10ml	vanilla flavouring/natural essence

Gradually fold dry ingredients into butter mixture. Because the cookie dough is very stiff, I find it easier to mix with a large spoon - wood, plastic or metal your choice. Just mix long enough to combine the ingredients, do not over-mix.

Using a tablespoon drop cookie dough by rounded portions 1½ to 2 inch (3-5cm) in size onto baking sheet 2 to 3 inches (5-8cm) apart. Bake for approximately 18 to 20 minutes for a soft centre cookie, slightly browned. Transfer cookies to a wire rack or cool surface.

Pecan Chocolate Chip Cookies . . . Mmmm, one of my favourites!

Pineapple Coconut Cookies

Preheat oven to Gas Mark 3 / 170°C / 325°F
This recipe will yield 18 to 24 cookies.

In a medium bowl add and combine with a fork or wire whisk

15oz / 425g	plain flour
½ teaspoon / 2.5ml	bicarbonate of soda

In large bowl cream butter, sugar, and flavouring. Scrape down the sides of
the bowl, add egg, pineapple & juice blend well

6oz /175g	dark brown sugar
5oz /150g	soft Demerara sugar
8oz / 225g	butter, softened
1	large egg
2 teaspoons / 10ml	vanilla flavouring/natural essence
1 Tablespoon / 15ml	pineapple juice
8oz / 225g	crushed pineapple, drained

Topping: 2oz / 60g   sweetened shredded coconut

Gradually fold dry ingredients into butter mixture. Because the cookie dough
is very stiff, I find it easier to mix with a large spoon - wood, plastic or metal
your choice. Just mix long enough to combine the ingredients, do not
over-mix.

Using a tablespoon drop cookie dough by rounded portions 1 ½ to 2 inch (3-5cm) in size
onto baking sheet 2 to 3 inches (5-8cm) apart. Flatten slightly and sprinkle with
shredded coconut. Bake for approximately 18 to 20 minutes for a soft centre cookie
slightly browned. Allow cookies to stand for one or two minutes to firm up before
removing from the baking sheet. Transfer cookies to a wire rack or cool surface.

*Whenever I
make these I
think of the four
months that I
spent in Hawaii
serving Uncle
Sam, boy was
that tough duty!*

Tangy Lemon Squares
Attention lemon meringue pie lovers . . . this one is for you!

Preheat oven to Gas Mark 4 / 180°C / 350°F
Grease an 8x8x2inch square baking tin

Pastry

5oz /140g	plain flour
4oz / 115g	butter, soft
2oz / 60g	icing sugar
1 teaspoon / 5ml	vanilla flavouring/natural essence

Filling

6oz / 175g	granulated sugar
1 Tablespoon / 15ml	plain flour
½ teaspoon / 2.5ml	baking powder
2	large eggs
2	lemons, grated zest and juice

Topping   Icing Sugar

Pastry: In a medium bowl, cream butter, sugar and vanilla until fluffy. Gradually add flour, mixing until well combined. Spread evenly into the bottom of the prepared baking pan building up ½ inch (12mm) edges, I like using my fingers for this job!

Bake pastry on the centre rack of oven for 20 minutes.

Filling: While pastry is baking, in a medium bowl, beat eggs for about 2 minutes, gradually add sugar, flour, baking powder, lemon zest and juice. You should finish your filling just about the time the pastry comes out of the oven. If you are ahead of yourself, relax, have a cuppa!

Pour mixture evenly over hot pastry, return to centre rack of oven for another 18-24 minutes or until filling is set and lightly browned. DO NOT OVERBAKE.

Cool on wire rack, top with icing sugar and cut into snack size 2inch (5cm) squares or for a rich delicious dessert, cut into larger pieces and serve with cream or a dollop of whipped cream - Mmmmm!

Variation:
Try substituting the lemons with a medium to large orange.

Cookie Notes

Muffins

Making Muffins ~ The Basics

Just like cookies, muffins are fun and easy to do! Muffins can be prepared and baked in less than one hour. And just like the cookies, they don't necessarily require expensive ingredients or special equipment, other than a muffin pan. However, you will need a few basic items.

The good news is you won't need an electric mixer and/or a food processor as muffin ingredients are easily mixed the old fashion way . . . by hand. So let's assume that you have already acquired mixing bowls, measuring spoons, measuring cup, scale, spatula and a wire whisk. Now all you need is a muffin pan!

Muffins are extremely easy to make, however, like cookies they take a little organization. Once again before starting, roll up your sleeves (ok, if you are wearing a sleeveless top or a T-shirt you can skip this part), put on your apron and wash your hands. Now just follow these simple steps for each recipe:

★ **Preheat oven.** Muffins bake best when they are put in a preheated oven. You know your oven; allow time (at least 15 minutes) for it to heat properly. Place rack in the middle of the oven.

★ **Prepare muffin pan.** Grease pan with butter, margarine or vegetable spray or use paper liners where recommended. I know this will sound silly but when I am not using paper liners with my non-stick muffin pans I usually grease them! For some reason the muffins just taste better.

★ **Assemble the ingredients.** Basically you want to have everything at hand that the recipe calls for. If you need to chop or grate any of the ingredients this is a good time to do it.

★ **Have your utensils at the ready;** two mixing bowls; one large, approximately 10 – 12 inches (25-30cm) in diameter; one medium bowl, approximately 8 – 10 inches (20-25cm) in diameter; a set of measuring cups; a set of measuring spoons; a wire whisk; a spatula and a large spoon.

★ **Measure wet ingredients** into the medium bowl. Add liquid to bowl together with butter or oil and egg(s). Combine well with whisk it is not necessary to beat mixture. If the recipe calls for fruit or vegetables add after you have combined wet ingredients. Set aside while mixing dry ingredients.

★ **Measure dry ingredients** into larger bowl. Add flour to bowl together with sugar, baking powder and/or bicarbonate of soda and spices and stir well with whisk (yes, the same whisk you used for the wet ingredients).

★ **Add wet ingredients to dry ingredients** all at once and fold together gently with the large spoon (trust me the whisk will not do the job as easy). Mix only until blended, consistency of batter will vary with recipe.

★ **Spoon batter into prepared muffin pan**. I usually fill the cups at least ¾ full. **Each recipe will make between 10 and 12 muffins.** If there is not enough batter to fill all the cups, the empty cups must be half filled with water. This will stop the pan from warping and it will add moisture to the muffins.

★ **Bake muffins** in the center of the oven, one pan at a time for even heat circulation. Muffins are done when the tops are lightly pressed and they spring back, if your finger leaves an indent continue baking for a few more minutes.

★ **Let muffins cool** slightly in pan and remove from pan within 10 minutes. Cool on wire rack before serving.

Don't panic it is not as complicated as it sounds. Basically you have two bowls, one for the dry ingredients and one for the wet ingredients. First you mix them separately and then you mix them together! Spoon the batter into the prepared muffin pan; bake them; cool them and eat them! It is as simple as that! Believe me once you have tried a few of the recipes you will be amazed at how quick and easy everything comes together.

Trust me, you do not have to be a rocket scientist to make great muffins. At the end of the day it is mostly common sense with a bit of general baking knowledge. But just in case you are lacking ever so slightly in either of these departments here are a few helpful hints:

★**The consistency** of the batter will vary by recipe. Whatever the consistency, a properly mixed batter produces a muffin with an even texture, with no large holes or tunnels. The muffin is moist and tender. An over-mixed batter brings out the gluten in the flour. This will produce an uneven texture, with large holes and tunnels. The muffin will be tough and dry.

★ **Oven**. All baking times & temperatures are for a conventional or gas oven. For a fan-assisted oven, the temperature should be reduced approximately 20˚C or one Gas Mark, also the baking time should be shortened by a few minutes. As oven temperatures can vary it is best to check your oven with an oven thermometer to ensure that the oven settings match the temperatures.

★ **Muffin Pans**. Please, please, please DO NOT use a shallow bun pan because "it wont work", get yourself a proper American muffin pan. A standard muffin pan has a cup that measures 2½" (7cm) X 1¼" (3cm). The other muffin pans that are now available are the mini and jumbo. Mini or jumbo muffins can be made from any batter. Mini muffin pans have cups that are 1 ½" (4cm) X 1" (2.5cm), reduce baking time to 10 to 15 minutes. The jumbo muffin pan cups are 3½"(9cm) X 1½"(3.5cm), increase baking time to 25 to 28 minutes.

★ **Flour.** All the recipes were tested with plain flour (store brand, works great and its inexpensive) measured straight from the package (sorry I don't sift). Flour absorption rates can vary as much as 20%, however, these variations will not make an appreciable difference in the finished product. Some of the recipes call for wholemeal plain flour, if you do not have any or you are not keen on wholemeal flour then substitute plain flour in equal amounts.

★ **Butter.** Butter or oil that is the question! Well, I prefer the flavour of butter, which is why the majority of recipes in this book call for it. Yes of course you can use margarine my preference here is baking margarine. And yes you can use oil. I prefer sunflower oil. I avoid "vegetable oils" because they are a blend of oils and will not always give successful muffins. In addition, you can sometimes end up with a slightly oily texture.

★ **Sugar**. Sugar adds sweetness, tenderness and moistness to recipes while it aids in browning. In general my preference is soft Demerara sugar it enhances the flavour without overpowering the other ingredients. White granulated sugar is a must for the fruit muffins as their flavour is so delicate.

★ **Milk.** Milk provides flavour and tenderness too. Most recipes work equally well with whole; semi-skimmed or skimmed milk. Powdered milk is a suitable substitute for fresh milk. An easy way to use powered milk is to substitute water for milk in the wet ingredients, add in the appropriate amount of powered milk with the dry ingredients. Also, if you want to boost your protein or calcium intake, double the amount of powered milk. This will enhance the nutritional value without affecting the texture or flavour. So use what you have on hand or what your diet dictates.

★ **Eggs.** The recipes in this book have been tested using large eggs. If you use a different size the recipe results may differ. Having said that, I have had equal success with medium eggs using 1 extra tablespoon of liquids. Don't be afraid to experiment.

★ **Flavouring.** Now I know this will upset the connoisseurs out there but most of the time I do use flavouring instead of natural essence. Why, well until just recently natural essence was not widely available so I have gotten in the habit of using the flavouring. Besides, the way my kids and their friends go through the muffins I honestly do not think they would know or appreciate the difference! Having said that I do use natural extract when I am baking for adults! Hey, I want to make a good impression!

★ **Baking powder and Bicarbonate of Soda**. Both of these are used as leaveners for many of the muffin recipes. Baking soda is used to neutralize acidic ingredients. Baking powder is not interchangeable with bicarbonate of soda.

OTHER TIPS

★ When doubling a recipe, cut back on seasonings such as salt, cinnamon, etc. If a single recipe calls for 1 teaspoon seasoning, for doubling only use 1½ teaspoons.

★ Remember, if you do not have enough batter to fill all the cups, fill remaining ones half full with water. This will add moisture to the muffins and stop the pan from burning.

★ Muffins are freezer friendly. Make sure that they have completely cooled before freezing. Place in airtight freezer bags or plastic containers. Store up to two months.

★ Muffins can be defrosted at room temperature. This usually takes about an hour of course this depends on the temperature of the room! Remove the muffins from the storage container, place on a plate and let stand until ready. Or if you have a pack-up, just wrap them up and they will be ready to eat later in the morning!

★ To reheat frozen or fresh muffins in a microwave, conventional or fan-assisted oven it is best to follow the manufacturer's owner's manual.

★ DO NOT refreeze muffins that have been thawed!

★ Muffins are at their best within two days of baking. Muffins should be stored in a container with a loose fitting lid as the muffin tops can become sticky or too moist in an airtight container.

★ If you prefer your muffins with a soft outside, use paper cup liners. Some of the recipes will call for them.

★Have you ever noticed how shiny objects reflect the sun's heat (*not that we have that much here in Britain*) and dull objects absorb it? Well, it is the same with muffin pans! Shiny pans actually reflect the heat, which means that the baking time will be a bit longer than dark or dull pans.

Hey, now that you know as much as I do . . . it is time to get started! No more excuses, get yourself in the kitchen and take control. Before you know it, your family and friends will be in awe of your muffins! No kidding!

Almond & Maraschino Cherry Muffins

Preheat oven to Gas Mark 6 / 200°C / 400°F
Prepare muffin pan

In a large bowl add and combine with a fork or wire whisk

12oz / 350g	plain flour
5oz / 150g	white granulated sugar
1 Tablespoon / 15ml	baking powder
½ teaspoon / 2.5ml	bicarbonate of soda
½ teaspoon / 2.5ml	salt
2oz / 60g	flaked almonds

For this recipe you will need one 225g jar of Maraschino Cocktail Cherries.
Drain cherry juice into measuring cup, add enough milk to bring up to 4fl oz / 120ml,
set aside. Cut cherries in half, set aside.

In a medium bowl add and combine with a wire whisk

2 large eggs	lightly beaten
4fl oz / 120ml	cherry juice & milk
4fl oz / 120ml	soured cream or plain natural yogurt
3oz / 85g	butter, melted
½ teaspoon / 2.5ml	almond flavouring/ natural essence
	Maraschino Cherries, halved

Gradually fold wet ingredients into dry ingredients. Fold in with a large spoon or rubber spatula until combined, do not over-mix.

Spoon batter into 10 of the prepared muffin cups, fill to the top of each cup; this will give a nice full sized muffin. Fill remaining cups half full with water to avoid burning the muffin pan and to give muffins moisture while baking.

Sprinkle tops with flaked almonds 1oz / 25g should do, bake for 20 to 25 minutes or until the tops spring back when gently touched. DO NOT OVER BAKE.
Allow to stand for one or two minutes, turn out on wire rack to cool.

As kids, whenever mom took us out to dinner we would always have our favourite drink . . . a "Roy Rogers" this was a Coke with grenadine and a maraschino cherry! We always thought it was an awesome drink . . . hey, we were only little and it made us feel grown up!

Apple, Rolled Oats & Raisin Muffins

Preheat oven to Gas Mark 5 / 190°C / 375°F
And prepare muffin pan or use paper liners

In a large bowl add and combine with a fork or wire whisk

6oz / 175g	plain flour
4oz / 115g	wholemeal plain flour
2oz / 60g	rolled or quick oats (not instant)
1 Tablespoon / 15ml	baking powder
½ teaspoon / 2.5ml	bicarbonate of soda
½ teaspoon / 2.5ml	salt
1 teaspoon / 5ml	ground cinnamon
½ teaspoon / 2.5ml	ground nutmeg

In a medium bowl add and combine with a wire whisk

2	large eggs, lightly beaten
4fl oz / 120ml	milk
4fl oz / 120ml	plain natural yogurt
4oz / 115g	butter, melted
4oz / 115g	dark brown sugar
3oz / 85g	Raisins (*humour me, use Californian!*)
1	medium to large baking apple peeled, cored and chopped

Gradually fold wet ingredients into dry ingredients. Fold in with a large spoon or rubber spatula until combined, do not over-mix.

Spoon batter into prepared muffin cups, fill to the top of each cup; this will give a nice full sized muffin.

Bake for 18 to 24 minutes or until tops spring back when gently touched. DO NOT OVER BAKE. Allow to stand for one or two minutes, turn out on wire rack to cool.

Grandma's favourite breakfast muffin!

Apple & Oriental Spice Muffins

Preheat oven to Gas Mark 5 / 190°C / 375°F
And prepare muffin pan or use paper liners

In a large bowl add and combine with a fork or wire whisk

12oz / 350g	plain flour
1 Tablespoon / 15ml	baking powder
½ teaspoon / 2.5ml	bicarbonate of soda
½ teaspoon / 2.5ml	salt
2 teaspoons / 10ml	Oriental Spice Powder

In medium bowl add and combine with a wire whisk
Add chopped apple last

2	large eggs, lightly beaten
6fl oz / 175ml	milk
3fl oz / 85ml	pure sunflower oil
4oz / 115g	dark brown sugar
1 teaspoon / 5ml	vanilla flavouring/ natural essence
6oz / 175g	apple, peeled & chopped

TOPPING:

2 teaspoons / 10ml	Oriental Spice Powder
2 teaspoons / 10ml	white granulated sugar

Gradually fold wet ingredients into dry ingredients. Fold in with a large spoon or rubber spatula until combined, do not over-mix.

Spoon batter into 10 / 11 of the prepared muffin cups, fill to the top of each cup; this will give a nice full sized muffin. Fill remaining cups half full with water to avoid burning the muffin pan and to give muffins moisture while baking.

Combine sugar & spice and sprinkle on tops bake for 20 to 25 minutes or until tops spring back when gently touched. DO NOT OVER BAKE.   Allow to stand for one or two minutes, turn out on wire rack to cool or just eat one because they smell sooo good!

TIP: Makes a great dessert when served with plain natural yogurt!
You will have to get the Oriental Spice Powder from a speciality shop, or you can try using Mixed Spice which is readily available at most supermarkets.

DO NOT USE Chinese 5 Spice.

In the 1800's the Chinese were instrumental in building the railways across the Great Plains to California, with the majority of them settling in San Francisco. The area they lived in soon became known as "Chinatown". San Francisco's "Chinatown" once boasted the world's largest Chinese population outside of mainland China! Needless to say our Chinese friends have had a big influence on the "City by the Bay!"

Banana Spice Muffins
These are great as a midday snack!

Preheat oven to Gas Mark 6 / 200°C / 400°F
And prepare muffin pan or use paper liners

In a large bowl add and combine with a fork or wire whisk

12oz / 350g	plain flour
1 Tablespoon / 15ml	baking powder
½ teaspoon / 2.5ml	salt
½ teaspoon / 2.5ml	ground ginger
½ teaspoon / 2.5ml	ground cinnamon
¼ teaspoon / 1.2ml	ground nutmeg (a good pinch)

In a medium bowl add and combine with a wire whisk

2	large eggs, lightly beaten
8fl oz / 240ml	milk
6oz / 175g	soft Demerara sugar
4oz / 115g	butter, melted
1 teaspoon / 5ml	vanilla flavouring/ natural essence
2 medium bananas	mashed but still chunky

Gradually fold wet ingredients into dry ingredients. Fold in with a large spoon or rubber spatula until combined, do not over-mix.

Spoon batter into the prepared muffin cups, fill to the top of each cup; this will give a nice full sized muffin. Bake for 18 to 24 minutes or until tops spring back when gently touched. DO NOT OVER BAKE.   Allow to stand for one or two minutes, turn out on wire rack to cool.

TIP: Remember, don't use your feet to mash the bananas!

Blueberry Muffins
One of my all time favourites!

Preheat oven to Gas Mark 5 / 190°C / 375°F
And prepare muffin pan or use paper liners

In a large bowl add and combine with a fork or wire whisk

12oz / 350g	plain flour
5oz / 150g	white granulated sugar
1 Tablespoon / 15ml	baking powder
½ teaspoon / 2.5ml	salt

In a medium bowl add and combine with a wire whisk
Add blueberries after you have combined the wet and dry ingredients

2	large eggs, lightly beaten
6fl oz / 175ml	milk
4oz / 115g	butter, melted
1 teaspoon / 5ml	vanilla flavouring / natural essence
7oz / 200g	fresh or frozen blueberries (if using frozen do not thaw)

Gradually fold wet ingredients into dry ingredients. Fold in with a large spoon or rubber spatula until combined, do not over-mix.

Spoon batter into 10 of the prepared muffin cups, fill to the top of each cup; this will give a nice full sized muffin. Fill remaining cups half full with water to avoid burning the muffin pan and to give muffins moisture while baking.

Sprinkle tops with white granulated sugar bake for 20 to 25 minutes or until or tops spring back when gently touched. DO NOT OVER BAKE.   Allow to stand for one or two minutes, turn out on wire rack to cool.

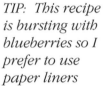

TIP: This recipe is bursting with blueberries so I prefer to use paper liners with this one!

Cheddar Mustard Muffins
These go great with a bowl of soup or a nice green salad!

Preheat oven to Gas Mark 6 / 200°C / 400°F
Prepare muffin pan or use paper liners

In a large bowl add and combine with a fork or wire whisk

12oz / 350g	plain flour
1 Tablespoon / 15ml	baking powder
1 Tablespoon / 15ml	white granulated sugar
½ teaspoon / 2.5ml	salt
¼ teaspoon / 1.2ml	coarse ground black pepper

In a medium bowl add and combine with a wire whisk

2	large eggs, lightly beaten
7fl oz / 200ml	milk
4oz / 115g	strong (#4 or #5) cheddar cheese
2oz / 60g	butter, melted
3 Tablespoons / 45ml	Dijon or Wholegrain Mustard

Variation: Apple Cheddar; omit coarse ground black pepper and mustard; add 6oz / 175g peeled, chopped apple.

Gradually fold wet ingredients into dry ingredients. Fold in with a large spoon or rubber spatula until combined, do not over-mix.

Spoon batter into 10/11 of the prepared muffin cups, fill to the top of each cup this will give a nice full sized muffin. Fill remaining cups half full with water to avoid burning the muffin pan and to give muffins moisture while baking.

Bake for 20 to 25 minutes or until tops spring back when gently touched. DO NOT OVER BAKE.   Allow to stand for one or two minutes, turn out on wire rack to cool.

Chunky Cookie Muffins

Use your favourite cream cookie (ok, biscuit!).

Preheat oven to Gas Mark 5 / 190°C / 375°F
And prepare muffin pan or use paper liners

In a large bowl add and combine with a fork or wire whisk

12oz / 350g	plain flour
1 Tablespoon / 15ml	baking powder
½ teaspoon / 2.5ml	salt
½ teaspoon / 2.5ml	bicarbonate of soda
8	Bourbon Creams broken up

In a medium bowl add and combine with a wire whisk

2	large eggs, lightly beaten
4fl oz / 120ml	plain natural yogurt
4fl oz / 120ml	milk
6oz / 175g	soft Demerara sugar
4oz / 115g	butter, melted
1 teaspoon / 5ml	vanilla flavouring / natural essence

Gradually fold wet ingredients into dry ingredients. Fold in with a large spoon or rubber spatula until combined, do not over-mix.

Spoon batter into 10 of the prepared muffin cups, fill to the top of each cup; this will give a nice full sized muffin. Fill remaining cups half full with water to avoid burning the muffin pan and to give muffins moisture while baking.

Bake for 20 to 25 minutes or until tops spring back when gently touched. DO NOT OVER BAKE.   Allow to stand for one or two minutes, turn out on wire rack to cool.

This recipe is just a bit of fun, you know breaking up cookies and then making something out of it! My kids think that it is weird to make muffins out of cookies, but they sure like the taste of them!

Citrus Surprise Muffins

Preheat oven to Gas Mark 5 / 190°C / 375°F
And prepare muffin pan or use a paper liner

In a large bowl add and combine with a fork or wire whisk

12oz / 350g	plain flour
1 Tablespoon / 15ml	baking powder
½ teaspoon / 2.5ml	bicarbonate of soda
½ teaspoon / 2.5ml	salt
Good pinch	ground nutmeg

In a medium bowl add and combine with a wire whisk
Add grated zucchini & carrot last

Check it out . . . these muffins have lemon, orange, carrot and zucchini (OK courgette to you!), and are topped with shredded coconut.
What an awesome combination!
These little babies won't last long at all!

2	large eggs, lightly beaten
5 oz / 150g	soft Demerara sugar
4fl oz / 120ml	pure sunflower oil
1	Lemon, grated zest and juice
1 medium	Orange, grated zest and juice
4oz / 115g	Zucchini, unpeeled but grated (Ok, Ok . . .courgette!)
4oz / 115g	Carrot, peeled and grated

Topping: Sweetened shredded coconut

Gradually fold wet ingredients into dry ingredients. Fold in with a large spoon or rubber spatula until combined, do not over-mix.

Spoon batter into the prepared muffin cups, fill to the top of each cup; this will give a nice full sized muffin. Top with shredded coconut.

Bake for 20 to 25 minutes or until tops spring back when gently touched. DO NOT OVER BAKE.   Allow to stand for one or two minutes, turn out on wire rack to cool.

TIP: A medium size carrot and a medium size courgette will do the job.

Classic Maple Pecan Muffins

Preheat oven to Gas Mark 6 / 200°C / 400°F
And prepare muffin pan or use paper liners

In a large bowl add and combine with a fork or wire whisk

8oz / 225g	plain flour
4oz / 115g	wholemeal plain flour
1 Tablespoon / 15ml	baking powder
½ teaspoon / 2.5ml	bicarbonate of soda
½ teaspoon / 2.5ml	salt
2oz / 60g	chopped pecans
2oz / 60g	soft Demerara sugar

In a medium bowl add and combine with a wire whisk

2	large eggs, lightly beaten
4fl oz / 120ml	milk
4fl oz / 120ml	soured cream
4fl oz / 120ml	pure maple syrup
3oz / 85g	butter, melted

Gradually fold wet ingredients into dry ingredients. Fold in with a large spoon or rubber spatula until combined, do not over-mix. This batter is a bit runny, don't worry you will have some great muffins.

Spoon batter into the prepared muffin cups, fill to the top of each cup; this will give a nice full sized muffin.

Place one or two pecan halves on top bake for 18 to 24 minutes or until tops spring back when gently touched. DO NOT OVER BAKE.   Allow to stand for one or two minutes, turn out on wire rack to cool.

☆ ☆ ☆ ☆ ☆ ☆ ☆ ☆ ☆

Canada is famous the world over for its maple syrup. Legend has it that Daniel Boone the frontiersman traded a Canadian tracker several muffin recipes for a jug of pure maple syrup! Americans love maple syrup on their pancakes and waffles, the muffins aren't bad either!

Coconut, Pineapple & Cherry Muffins

Preheat oven to Gas Mark 5 / 190°C / 375°F
And prepare muffin pan or use paper liners

In a large bowl add and combine with a fork or wire whisk

12oz / 350g	plain flour
1 Tablespoon / 15ml	baking powder
½ teaspoon / 2.5ml	bicarbonate of soda
½ teaspoon / 2.5ml	salt

For this recipe you will need one 225g jar of Maraschino Cocktail Cherries.
Drain cherry juice into measuring cup. Cut cherries in half, set aside.

In a medium bowl add and combine with a wire whisk

2	large eggs, lightly beaten
3oz / 85g	butter, melted
2oz / 60g	dark brown sugar
4 Tablespoons / 60ml	maraschino cherry juice
8fl oz / 240ml	crushed pineapple with juice
1 teaspoon / 5ml	almond flavouring/ natural essence
2oz / 60g	shredded sweetened coconut
	maraschino cherries, halved

TOPPING: Shredded Coconut

Gradually fold wet ingredients into dry ingredients. Fold in with a large spoon or rubber spatula until combined, do not over-mix.

Spoon batter into the prepared muffin cups, fill to the top of each cup; this will give a nice full sized muffin.

Sprinkle tops with shredded coconut bake for 18 to 24 minutes or until tops spring back when gently touched. DO NOT OVER BAKE.   Allow to stand for one or two minutes, turn out on wire rack to cool.

Close your eyes as you take your first bite and just picture yourself laying on a beach in Hawaii!

Courgette Spice Muffins

Preheat oven to Gas Mark 6 / 200°C / 400°F
And prepare muffin pan or use paper liners

In a large bowl add and combine with a fork or wire whisk

6oz / 175g	plain flour
6oz / 175g	wholemeal plain flour
1 Tablespoon / 15ml	baking powder
½ teaspoon / 2.5ml	bicarbonate of soda
½ teaspoon / 2.5ml	salt
1 teaspoon / 5ml	ground cinnamon
¼ teaspoon / 1.2ml	ground nutmeg
2oz / 60g	chopped walnuts

In a medium bowl add and combine with a wire whisk
Add grated courgette last

2	large eggs, lightly beaten
4fl oz / 120ml	milk
4fl oz / 120ml	pure sunflower oil
6oz / 175g	soft Demerara sugar
1 teaspoon / 5ml	vanilla flavouring/ natural essence
8oz / 225g	unpeeled grated courgette (happy?!)

TOPPING: 1oz / 25g chopped walnut

Gradually fold wet ingredients into dry ingredients. Fold in with a large spoon or rubber spatula until combined, do not over-mix.

Spoon batter into 10 / 11 of the prepared muffin cups, fill to the top of each cup; this will give a nice full sized muffin. Fill remaining cups half full with water to avoid burning the muffin pan and to give muffins moisture while baking.

Sprinkle tops with chopped walnuts bake for 20 to 25 minutes or until tops spring back when gently touched. DO NOT OVER BAKE.   Allow to stand for one or two minutes, turn out on wire rack to cool.

You say courgette, I say zucchini, you say tomato . . . do you get my meaning! You know I believe it was Winston Churchill that said "We are two great nations separated by a common language!"

Delightful Corn Muffins

Preheat oven to Gas Mark 5 / 190°C / 375°F
And prepare muffin pan or use paper liners

In a large bowl add and combine with a fork or wire whisk

6oz / 175g	plain flour
6oz / 175g	maize flour
4oz / 115g	white granulated sugar
1 Tablespoon / 15ml	baking powder
½ teaspoon / 2.5ml	salt

In a medium bowl add and combine with a wire whisk

2	large eggs, lightly beaten
8fl oz / 240ml	milk
4oz / 115g	butter, melted

Gradually fold wet ingredients into dry ingredients. Fold in with a large spoon or rubber spatula until combined, do not over-mix.

Spoon batter into 10 of the prepared muffin cups, fill to the top of each cup; this will give a nice full sized muffin. Fill remaining cups half full with water to avoid burning the muffin pan and to give muffins moisture while baking.

Bake for 16 to 20 minutes or until tops spring back when gently touched. DO NOT OVER BAKE.   Allow to stand for one or two minutes, turn out on wire rack to cool.

TIP: Living in the North of England I find that cornmeal is not widely available which is why I use Maize Flour. Maize Flour is available through most health food stores. If you want a more grainy texture use Polenta (Italian cornmeal) in the same amount.

Honest they are delightful, serve them with a full English fry up, warm with butter and honey!
You will never want fried bread again.

Double Chocolate Chip Muffins

Preheat oven to Gas Mark 5 / 190°C / 375°F
And prepare muffin pan
(Do not use paper liners with this one!)

In a large bowl add and combine with a fork or wire whisk

12oz / 350g	plain flour
3oz / 85g	unsweetened cocoa powder
7oz / 200g	plain chocolate chips (2 100g packs)
1 Tablespoon / 15ml	baking powder
½ teaspoon / 2.5ml	bicarbonate soda
½ teaspoon / 2.5ml	salt

In a medium bowl add and combine with a wire whisk.

2	large eggs, lightly beaten
4fl oz / 120ml	plain natural yogurt
4fl oz / 120ml	milk plus 1 Tablespoon
6oz / 175g	butter, melted
7oz / 200g	soft Demerara sugar
1 teaspoon / 5ml	vanilla essence / natural flavouring

Gradually fold wet ingredients into dry ingredients. Fold in with a large spoon or rubber spatula until combined, do not over-mix.

Spoon batter into the prepared muffin cups, fill to the top of each cup; this will give a nice full sized muffin.

Bake for 18 to 24 minutes or until tops spring back when gently touched. DO NOT OVER BAKE.   Allow to stand for one or two minutes, turn out on wire rack to cool or just eat one because they smell sooo good!

Variation: How about some chopped walnuts – 2oz / 50g would do nicely. Or how about a **Triple Chocolate Muffin**, substitute a 150g bar of White Chocolate coarse chopped for one pack of plain chocolate chips!

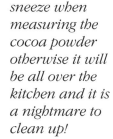

Attention chocoholics. . . this one is for you! Don't be alarmed. . . these muffins have a very robust top!

TIP: DO NOT sneeze when measuring the cocoa powder otherwise it will be all over the kitchen and it is a nightmare to clean up!

Fresh Lemon & Ginger Muffins

The only way to describe this muffin is sweet and tangy!

Preheat oven to Gas Mark 5 / 190°C / 375°F
And prepare muffin pan or use paper liners

In a large bowl add and combine with a fork or wire whisk

12oz / 350g	plain flour
7oz / 200g	white granulated sugar
1 Tablespoon / 15ml	baking powder
½ teaspoon / 2.5ml	bicarbonate of soda
½ teaspoon / 2.5ml	salt

In a medium bowl add and combine with a wire whisk

2	large eggs, lightly beaten
4fl oz / 120ml	milk
4fl oz / 120ml	plain natural yogurt
4oz / 115g	butter, melted
3 Tablespoons / 45ml	fresh ginger root, peeled & chopped
2	Lemons, grated rind only

TOPPING: In a small bowl mix juice from the 2 lemons with
2 Tablespoons / 30ml   white granulated sugar.

Gradually fold wet ingredients into dry ingredients. Fold in with a large spoon or rubber spatula until combined, do not over-mix.

Spoon batter into 10 / 11 of the prepared muffin cups, fill to the top of each cup; this will give a nice full sized muffin. Fill remaining cups half full with water to avoid burning the muffin pan and to give muffins moisture while baking.

Bake for 18 to 24 minutes or until tops spring back when gently touched. DO NOT OVER BAKE.   Allow to stand for one or two minutes, as you remove muffins from the pan dip the tops into the lemon juice mixture, place on wire rack to cool.

TIP: If you are pressed for time, instead of fresh ginger root why not try prepared ginger. It is quick and easy to use, just make sure you drain off the liquid!

Hazelnut Pineapple Banana Muffins

Here is a nutty tropical treat!

Preheat oven to Gas Mark 6 / 200°C / 400°F
And prepare muffin pan or use paper liners

In a large bowl add and combine with a fork or wire whisk

6oz / 175g	plain flour
4oz / 115g	wholemeal plain flour
2oz / 60g	rolled oats
1 Tablespoon / 15ml	baking powder
½ teaspoon / 2.5ml	bicarbonate of soda
½ teaspoon / 2.5ml	salt
1 teaspoon / 5ml	ground cinnamon
3oz / 100g	chopped hazelnuts
	set aside half for topping.

In a medium bowl add and combine with a wire whisk

2	large eggs, lightly beaten
4fl oz / 120ml	plain natural yogurt
3fl oz / 85ml	pineapple juice
4oz / 115g	butter, melted
6oz / 175g	pineapple pieces, drained and cut in half
1 large or 2 medium	bananas peeled and diced

TOPPING: Chopped hazelnuts

Gradually fold wet ingredients into dry ingredients. Fold in with a large spoon or rubber spatula until combined, do not over-mix.

Spoon batter into the prepared muffin cups, fill to the top of each cup; this will give a nice full sized muffin. Sprinkle tops with chopped hazelnuts.

Bake for 18 to 24 minutes or until tops spring back when gently touched. DO NOT OVER BAKE.   Allow to stand for one or two minutes, turn out on wire rack to cool.

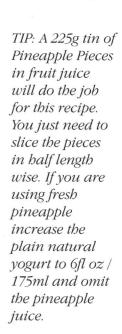

TIP: A 225g tin of Pineapple Pieces in fruit juice will do the job for this recipe. You just need to slice the pieces in half length wise. If you are using fresh pineapple increase the plain natural yogurt to 6fl oz / 175ml and omit the pineapple juice.

Lainey's Raspberry Muffins with Nutty Topping

Preheat oven to Gas Mark 6 / 200°C / 400°F
Prepare muffin pan or use paper liners

In a large bowl add and combine with a fork or wire whisk

12oz / 350g	plain flour
7oz / 200g	white granulated sugar
1 Tablespoon / 15ml	baking powder
½ teaspoon / 2.5ml	bicarbonate of soda
½ teaspoon / 2.5ml	salt

In a medium bowl add and combine with a wire whisk
Add raspberries after you have combined the wet & dry ingredients

2	large eggs, lightly beaten
4fl oz / 120ml	milk
4fl oz / 120ml	plain natural yogurt
3fl oz / 85ml	pure sunflower oil
1 medium orange	grated zest only
5oz / 150g	raspberries, fresh or frozen (if frozen do not thaw).

Topping: In a small bowl add and combine

2oz / 60g	chopped pecans or hazelnuts
1oz / 25g	dark brown sugar
2 Tablespoon / 30ml	plain flour
1 Tablespoon / 15ml	butter, melted

Gradually fold wet ingredients into dry ingredients. Fold in with a large spoon or rubber spatula until combined, do not over-mix.

Spoon batter into the prepared muffin cups, fill to the top of each cup; this will give a nice full sized muffin.

Sprinkle topping on each cup bake for 20 to 25 minutes or until tops spring back when gently touched. DO NOT OVER BAKE.   Allow to stand for one or two minutes, turn out on wire rack to cool or just eat one because they smell sooo good!

When I had the restaurant a wonderful lady by the name of Elaine Clarke used to help me in the kitchen (actually she did most of the work). As much as I hate to admit it, her Raspberry Muffins always seemed better than mine! So I promised her when I did the book these would be named in her honour!

☆ ☆ ☆ ☆ ☆ ☆ ☆ ☆ ☆

Lemon Poppy Seed Muffins

I hate to say it, but these go great with a cuppa,
I think that I have been in England too long!

Preheat oven to Gas Mark 6 / 200°C / 400°F
And prepare muffin pan or use paper liners

In a large bowl add and combine with a fork or wire whisk

12oz / 350g	plain flour
1 Tablespoon / 15ml	baking powder
½ teaspoon / 2.5ml	bicarbonate of soda
½ teaspoon / 2.5ml	salt
1oz / 25g	poppy seeds
5oz / 150g	white granulated sugar

In a medium bowl add and combine with a wire whisk

2	large eggs, lightly beaten
4fl oz / 120ml	natural plain yogurt
4oz / 115g	butter, melted
½ teaspoon / 2.5ml	lemon flavouring/ natural essence
2	lemons, grated zest and juice

Gradually fold wet ingredients into dry ingredients. Fold in with a large spoon or rubber spatula until combined, do not over-mix.

Spoon batter into the prepared muffin cups, fill to the top of each cup; this will give a nice full sized muffin.

Bake for 18 to 24 minutes or until tops spring back when gently touched. DO NOT OVER BAKE.   Allow to stand for one or two minutes, turn out on wire rack to cool.

So I said, "Mom I have made some Lemon Poppy Seed Muffins" . . . she replied "you know I can't eat those, the poppy seeds don't get along at all with my false teeth!" Oops, sorry! (I wasn't really it just means more for me and the kids!)

Mama mia Pizza Muffins

Preheat oven to Gas Mark 6 / 200°C / 400°F
And prepare muffin pan or use paper liners

In a large bowl add and combine with a fork or wire whisk

7oz / 200g	plain flour
5oz / 150g	wholemeal plain flour
1 Tablespoon / 15ml	baking powder
1 Tablespoon / 15ml	white granulated sugar
½ teaspoon / 2.5ml	salt
1 teaspoon / 5ml	dried oregano

In a medium bowl add and combine with a wire whisk
except for the mozzarella cheese

2	large eggs, lightly beaten
4fl oz / 120ml	milk
4fl oz / 120ml	prepared pasta sauce
3fl oz / 85ml	extra virgin olive oil
4oz / 115g	mozzarella Cheese,
	cut into 20 cubes

Gradually fold wet ingredients into dry ingredients. Fold in with a large spoon or rubber spatula until combined, do not over-mix.

Spoon approximately 1 Tablespoon of batter into 10 / 11 of the prepared muffin cups; put a cube of cheese in each cup; cover with remaining batter. This will give a nice full sized muffin. Fill remaining cups half full with water to avoid burning the muffin pan and to give muffins moisture while baking.

Place a cube of cheese on the tops and bake for 18 to 24 minutes or until tops spring back when gently touched. DO NOT OVER BAKE.   Allow to stand for one or two minutes, turn out on wire rack to cool.

Variation: How about a slice of pepperoni halved on each top with the mozzarella cheese!

Here is a fantastic midday snack! When I told Maggie about these, she said "what's next dad . . . fish & chip muffins!" Hmmm, maybe!

☆ ☆ ☆ ☆ ☆ ☆ ☆ ☆ ☆ ☆

Muffin Mexicana

Preheat oven to Gas Mark 6 / 200°C / 400°F
And prepare muffin pan or use paper liners

In a large bowl add and combine with a fork or wire whisk

6oz / 175g	plain flour
6oz / 175g	maize flour or Polenta
1 Tablespoon / 15ml	baking powder
½ teaspoon / 2.5ml	bicarbonate soda
¼ teaspoon / 1.2ml	salt

In a medium bowl add and combine with a wire whisk

2	large eggs, lightly beaten
One Jar 226g	Hot & Thick Salsa
1 Tablespoon / 15ml	soft Demerara sugar
3oz / 85g	canned sweet corn, drained
3oz / 85g	strong cheddar cheese (#4 or #5)
3 Tablespoons / 45ml	pure sunflower oil

Gradually fold wet ingredients into dry ingredients. Fold in with a large spoon or rubber spatula until combined, do not over-mix.

Spoon batter into 10 of the prepared muffin cups, fill to the top of each cup; this will give a nice full sized muffin. Fill remaining cups half full with water to avoid burning the muffin pan and to give muffins moisture while baking.

Bake for 15 to 20 minutes or until tops spring back when gently touched. DO NOT OVER BAKE. Allow to stand for one or two minutes, turn out on wire rack to cool.

Variation: Hey, how about adding 3 or 4 chopped jalapeño peppers to the batter! That should warm your insides up.

Did you know that over 40% of California's population is from Central and South America! Needless to say our Hispanic friends have a big influence on California cuisine, which includes muffins!

Nutmeg, Pear & Hazelnut Muffins

Preheat oven to Gas Mark 5 / 190°C / 375°F
And prepare muffin pan or use paper liners

In a large bowl add and combine with a fork or wire whisk

12oz / 350g	plain flour
1 Tablespoon / 15ml	baking powder
½ teaspoon / 2.5ml	bicarbonate of soda
½ teaspoon / 2.5ml	salt
1 teaspoon / 5ml	ground nutmeg
2oz / 60g	chopped hazelnuts

In a medium bowl add and combine with a wire whisk

2	large eggs, lightly beaten
6fl oz / 175ml	plain natural yogurt
4oz / 115g	butter, melted
4oz / 115g	dark brown sugar
7oz / 200g	fresh pears, peeled & diced
1	lemon, grated zest only

Gradually fold wet ingredients into dry ingredients. Fold in with a large spoon or rubber spatula until combined, do not over-mix.

Spoon batter into the prepared muffin cups, fill to the top of each cup; this will give a nice full sized muffin.

Bake for 18 to 24 minutes or until tops spring back when gently touched. DO NOT OVER BAKE.   Allow to stand for one or two minutes, turn out on wire rack to cool.

TIP: Instead of fresh pears a 410g tin of pear halves drained will do the job perfectly!

Another delightful combination! I love to use nutmeg, it always brings up festive memories and the aroma is wonderful.

Nutty Peanut Butter
& Strawberry Jam Muffins

Preheat oven to Gas Mark 6 / 200°C / 400°F
And prepare muffin pan or use paper liners

In a large bowl add and combine with a fork or wire whisk

12oz / 350g	plain flour
1 Tablespoon / 15ml	baking powder
½ teaspoon / 2.5ml	salt

In a medium bowl add and combine with a wire whisk
Except for the Strawberry Jam

2	large eggs, lightly beaten
8fl oz / 240ml	milk
3oz / 85g	soft Demerara sugar
3oz / 85g	chunky peanut butter
4oz / 115g	butter, melted
1 teaspoon / 5ml	vanilla flavouring/ natural essence
4oz / 115g	Strawberry Jam

Gradually fold wet ingredients into dry ingredients. Fold in with a large spoon or rubber spatula until combined, do not over-mix.

Spoon approximately 1 Tablespoon batter into 10 of the prepared muffin cups, top with approximately 1 rounded teaspoon of strawberry jam; with remaining batter fill to the top of each cup; this will give a nice full sized muffin. Fill remaining cups half full with water to avoid burning the muffin pan and to give muffins moisture while baking.

Bake for 18 to 24 minutes or until tops spring back when gently touched. DO NOT OVER BAKE.   Allow to stand for one or two minutes, turn out on wire rack to cool.

Hey, the name alone is a mouthful! Peanut Butter and Jam sandwiches are to the Americans what beans on toast are to the Brits! But wait until you try these little gems!

Orange Chocolate Chip Muffins
What a great combination!

Preheat oven to Gas Mark 6 / 200°C / 400°F
And prepare muffin pan or use paper liners

In a large bowl add and combine with a fork or wire whisk

12oz / 350g	plain flour
5oz / 150g	white granulated sugar
7oz / 200g	plain chocolate chips (2 100g packs)
1 Tablespoon / 15ml	baking powder
½ teaspoon / 2.5ml	bicarbonate of soda
½ teaspoon / 2.5ml	salt

In a medium bowl add and combine with a wire whisk

2	large eggs, lightly beaten
2 medium oranges	grated zest
8fl oz / 240ml	combination milk & juice from 2 medium oranges
4oz / 115g	butter, melted

Gradually fold wet ingredients into dry ingredients. Fold in with a large spoon or rubber spatula until combined, do not over-mix.

Spoon batter into the prepared muffin cups, fill to the top of each cup; this will give a nice full sized muffin. Batter is a bit runny, don't worry your muffins will be great!

Sprinkle tops with white granulated sugar bake for 18 to 24 minutes or until tops spring back when gently touched. DO NOT OVER BAKE. Allow to stand for one or two minutes, turn out on wire rack to cool or just eat one because they smell sooo good!

Hey, have you tried the Orange Chocolate Chip Cookie?

Peachy Yogurt Muffins

Preheat oven to Gas Mark 6 / 200°C / 400°F
And prepare muffin pan or use paper liners

In a large bowl add and combine with a fork or wire whisk

8oz / 225g	plain flour
4oz / 115g	wholemeal plain flour
1 Tablespoon / 15ml	baking powder
½ teaspoon / 2.5ml	bicarbonate soda
½ teaspoon / 2.5ml	salt
½ teaspoon / 2.5ml	ground cinnamon

In a medium bowl add and combine with a fork or wire whisk;
Add peaches after combining other ingredients

2	large eggs, lightly beaten
8oz / 240ml	plain natural yogurt
3oz / 85g	butter, melted
3 Tablespoons / 45ml	honey
2oz / 60g	dark brown sugar
1 teaspoon / 5ml	vanilla flavouring /natural essence
6oz / 175g	fresh ripe peaches, peeled and chopped or canned peaches, drained and chopped

Gradually fold wet ingredients into dry ingredients. Fold in with a large spoon or rubber spatula until combined, do not over-mix.

Spoon batter into 11/12 of the prepared muffin cups, fill to the top of each cup; this will give a nice full sized muffin. Fill remaining cups half full with water to avoid burning the muffin pan and to give muffins moisture while baking.

Sprinkle tops with granulated sugar bake for 18 to 20 minutes or until tops spring back when gently touched. DO NOT OVER BAKE.   Allow to stand for one or two minutes, turn out on wire rack to cool.

Variation: How about some chopped pecans – 2oz / 60g would do nicely!

This one goes great with a cuppa any time of the day!

Peanut Butter Banana Muffins

Preheat oven to Gas Mark 5 / 190°C / 375°F
And prepare muffin pan or use paper liners

In a large bowl add and combine with a fork or wire whisk

10oz / 280g	plain flour
2oz / 60g	rolled or quick oats (not instant!)
1 Tablespoon / 15ml	baking powder

In a medium bowl add and combine with a wire whisk

2	large eggs, lightly beaten
8fl oz / 240ml	milk
4oz / 115g	peanut butter
2oz / 60g	butter, melted
3oz / 85g	dark brown sugar
1 teaspoon / 5ml	vanilla flavouring/ natural essence
2	Medium ripe bananas – coarse chopped

Gradually fold wet ingredients into dry ingredients. Fold in with a large spoon or rubber spatula until combined, do not over-mix.

Spoon batter into the prepared muffin cups, fill to the top of each cup; this will give a nice full sized muffin.

Bake for 18 to 24 minutes or until tops spring back when gently touched. DO NOT OVER BAKE. Allow to stand for one or two minutes, turn out on wire rack to cool.

TIP: It is easier to peel the bananas before you chop them than after! Hey you never know, some people have a lot of time on their hands and may not mind peeling each little piece!.

If you love peanut butter then this one is for you! You can use smooth or crunchy.

Prune & Rolled Oat Muffins

This one has lots of fibre . . . a great way to go!

Preheat oven to Gas Mark 6 / 200°C / 400°F
And prepare muffin pan or use paper liners

In a large bowl add and combine with a fork or wire whisk

8oz / 225g	plain flour
4oz / 115g	wholemeal plain flour
3oz / 85g	rolled oats
1 Tablespoon / 15ml	baking powder
½ teaspoon / 2.5ml	salt
1 teaspoon / 5ml	oriental spice

In a medium bowl add and combine with a wire whisk

2	large eggs, lightly beaten
8fl oz / 240ml	milk
4fl oz / 120ml	pure sunflower oil
2 teaspoons / 10ml	vanilla flavouring/ natural essence
3oz / 85g	dark brown sugar
3oz / 85g	soft Demerara sugar
6oz / 175g	chopped pitted prunes

TOPPING: In a small bowl combine 2 teaspoons / 10ml white granulated sugar and 1 teaspoon / 5ml oriental spice

Gradually fold wet ingredients into dry ingredients. Fold in with a large spoon or rubber spatula until combined, do not over-mix.

Spoon batter into the prepared muffin cups, fill to the top of each cup; this will give a nice full sized muffin. Sprinkle tops with sugar mixture.

Bake for 18 to 24 minutes or until tops spring back when gently touched. DO NOT OVER BAKE.   Allow to stand for one or two minutes, turn out on wire rack to cool.

You know all my friends tell me I'm a "regular guy", so if you want to be like me this is the muffin for you!

Rhubarb Cinnamon Muffins

Preheat oven to Gas Mark 5 / 190°C / 375°F
And prepare muffin pan or use paper liners

In a large bowl add and combine with a fork or wire whisk

8oz / 225g	plain flour
4oz / 115g	wholemeal plain flour
1 Tablespoon / 15ml	baking powder
½ teaspoon / 2.5ml	bicarbonate of soda
½ teaspoon / 2.5ml	salt
½ teaspoon / 2.5ml	ground cinnamon
¼ teaspoon / 1.2ml	ground nutmeg

In a medium bowl add and combine with a wire whisk

2	large eggs, lightly beaten
4fl oz / 120ml	milk
4fl oz / 120ml	plain natural yogurt
4fl oz / 120ml	pure sunflower oil
1 teaspoon / 5ml	vanilla flavouring/ natural essence
7oz / 200g	fresh rhubarb, coarse chopped

Gradually fold wet ingredients into dry ingredients. Fold in with a large spoon or rubber spatula until combined, do not over-mix.

Spoon batter into 10 / 11 of the prepared muffin cups, fill to the top of each cup; this will give a nice full sized muffin. Fill remaining cups half full with water to avoid burning the muffin pan and to give muffins moisture while baking.

Sprinkle with white granulated sugar bake for 20 to 25 minutes or until tops spring back when gently touched. DO NOT OVER BAKE. Allow to stand for one or two minutes, turn out on wire rack to cool.

Only fresh rhubarb will do, don't even think about using canned!

Rum & Raisin Muffins

Preheat oven to Gas Mark 6 / 200°C / 400°F
And prepare muffin pan or use paper liners

In a large bowl add and combine with a fork or wire whisk

12oz / 350g	plain flour
1 Tablespoon / 15ml	baking powder
½ teaspoon / 2.5ml	bicarbonate soda
½ teaspoon / 2.5ml	salt
½ teaspoon / 2.5ml	ground cinnamon
½ teaspoon / 2.5ml	ground nutmeg

In a medium bowl add and combine with a wire whisk
Add raisins after other ingredients have been combined

2	large eggs, lightly beaten
4fl oz / 120ml	milk
4fl oz / 120ml	soured cream
3oz / 85g	soft Demerara sugar
3oz / 85g	butter, melted
2 teaspoons / 10ml	rum flavouring or natural essence
4oz / 115g	raisins, Californian!

Gradually fold wet ingredients into dry ingredients. Fold in with a large spoon or rubber spatula until combined, do not over-mix.

Spoon batter into 10 / 11 of the prepared muffin cups, fill to the top of each cup; this will give a nice full sized muffin. Fill remaining cups half full with water to avoid burning the muffin pan and to give muffins moisture while baking.

Bake for 20 to 25 minutes or until tops spring back when gently touched. DO NOT OVER BAKE.   Allow to stand for one or two minutes, turn out on wire rack to cool.

Whenever anyone mentions Rum, I always think of the British Navy. A time of "wooden ships and iron men with their ration of Rum singing seafaring songs!" So here's a muffin for you "land lubbers".

Scrumptious Chocolate Chip Muffins

Mike's favourite, super moist . . . melt in your mouth not in your hand!

Preheat oven to Gas Mark 5 / 190°C / 375°F
And prepare muffin pan or use paper liners

In a large bowl add and combine with a fork or wire whisk

12oz / 350g	plain flour
7oz / 200g	plain chocolate chips
1 Tablespoon / 15ml	baking powder
½ teaspoon / 2.5ml	bicarbonate soda
½ teaspoon / 2.5ml	salt

In a medium bowl add and combine with a wire whisk

2	large eggs, lightly beaten
7oz / 200ml	plain natural yogurt
7oz / 200g	soft Demerara sugar
4oz / 115g	butter, melted
2 teaspoons / 10ml	vanilla flavouring or natural essence

Gradually fold wet ingredients into dry ingredients. Fold in with a large spoon or rubber spatula until combined, do not over-mix.

Spoon batter into 10 of the prepared muffin cups, fill to the top of each cup; this will give a nice full sized muffin. Fill remaining cups half full with water to avoid burning the muffin pan and to give muffins moisture while baking.

Bake for 20 to 25 minutes or until tops spring back when gently touched. DO NOT OVER BAKE. Allow to stand for one or two minutes, turn out on wire rack to cool.

The only way I can get Mike off his computer is to bake a batch of his favourite muffins, actually any muffins or cookies will do the trick!

The "Good Morning" Muffins

**Preheat oven to Gas Mark 5 / 190°C / 375°F
And use paper liners in the muffin pan**

In a large bowl add and combine with a fork or wire whisk

8oz / 225g	plain flour
4oz / 115g	wholemeal plain flour
2oz / 60g	chopped pecans
5oz 150g	soft Demerara sugar
1 Tablespoon / 15ml	baking powder
½ teaspoon / 2.5ml	salt
2 teaspoons / 10ml	ground cinnamon

In a medium bowl add and combine with a wire whisk

3	large eggs, lightly beaten
4oz / 115g	butter, melted
7oz / 200g	carrots, peeled and grated (2 medium should do it)
3oz / 85g	raisins
1oz / 25g	shredded coconut (sweetened)
1	Large baking apple peeled, cored and grated
2 teaspoon / 10ml	vanilla flavouring/ natural essence

Gradually fold wet ingredients into dry ingredients. Fold in with a large spoon or rubber spatula until combined, because of the large volume of grated carrots and apple this one takes a bit effort to mix.

Spoon batter into the prepared muffin cups, fill to the top of each cup; this will give a nice full sized muffin. Again because of the volume of this batter you may actually slightly overfill the cups. Keep the batter within the paper cup liner and it should be fine. Always works for me!

Bake for 20 to 25 minutes or until tops spring back when gently touched. DO NOT OVER BAKE.   Allow to stand for one or two minutes, turn out on wire rack to cool.

☆ ☆ ☆ ☆ ☆ ☆ ☆ ☆ ☆

These little babies have carrots, apples, raisins, pecans & coconut . . . another awesome combination! A couple of these down your neck in the morning with a cuppa and you are set until lunch!

Traditional Mincemeat Muffins

Preheat oven to Gas Mark 6 / 200°C / 400°F
And prepare muffin pan or use paper liners

In a large bowl add and combine with a fork or wire whisk

12oz / 350g	plain flour
1 Tablespoon / 15ml	baking powder
½ teaspoon / 2.5ml	bicarbonate soda
½ teaspoon / 2.5ml	salt
3oz / 85g	soft Demerara sugar

In a medium bowl add and combine with a wire whisk

2	large eggs, lightly beaten
4fl oz / 120ml	soured cream
4fl oz / 120ml	milk
3oz / 85g	butter, melted
13oz / 375g	ready made mincemeat; a 411g jar will do the trick!
2 medium oranges	grated zest only

TOPPING: 1oz / 25g chopped walnuts

Gradually fold wet ingredients into dry ingredients. Fold in with a large spoon or rubber spatula until combined, do not over-mix.

Spoon batter into 10 / 11 of the prepared muffin cups, fill to the top of each cup; this will give a nice full sized muffin. Fill remaining cups half full with water to avoid burning the muffin pan and to give muffins moisture while baking.

Sprinkle tops with chopped walnuts 1oz / 25g should do the job nicely. Bake for 20 to 25 minutes or until tops spring back when gently touched. DO NOT OVER BAKE. Allow to stand for one or two minutes, turn out on wire rack to cool.

It seems that some form of this recipe always appears in newspapers and magazines around Thanksgiving & Christmas time, hence "Traditional". But they are good any time of the year!

Upside Down Pecan Muffins

Preheat oven to Gas Mark 6 / 200°C / 400°F
**Prepare muffin pan, pay attention now, this one is upside down
so you do not use paper liners!**

Ok, the first thing we need to do is spoon 1 Tablespoon of melted butter in each muffin cup. Now place 4 pecan halves in a single layer in each cup; next spoon about I teaspoon of dark brown sugar into each cup on top of the nuts.

48 pecan halves	One 100g pack, there will be some left over
4oz / 115g	butter
4oz / 115g	dark brown sugar

In a large bowl add and combine with a fork or wire whisk

10oz / 280g	plain flour
1 Tablespoon / 15ml	baking powder
½ teaspoon / 2.5ml	bicarbonate of soda
½ teaspoon / 2.5ml	salt
1 teaspoon / 5ml	ground cinnamon
½ teaspoon / 2.5ml	ground nutmeg

In a medium bowl add and combine with a wire whisk

2	large eggs, lightly beaten
4fl oz / 120ml	natural yogurt or soured cream
4fl oz / 120ml	milk
2oz / 60g	butter, melted, cooled
3oz / 85g	dark brown sugar
1 teaspoon / 5ml	vanilla flavouring/natural essence

Gradually fold wet ingredients into dry ingredients. Fold in with a large spoon or rubber spatula until combined, do not over-mix. Spoon batter over brown sugar mixture, dividing it evenly and gently work the batter to the sides of each cup to create a seal. This will stop or slow down the butter mixture from bubbling out. Bake for 15 to 18 mintues or until tops spring back when gently touched.

Now, gently run a knife or small spatula around each cup to loosen the muffin. Place a baking tray of equal size over the pan, turn it over, tap each cup and lift off pan; muffins will now be standing upside down! Allow to cool for a few minutes before serving.

These are Maggie's all time favourites. I make them for her every Sunday morning!

Walnut & Boursin Cheese Muffins

Here's another one that goes great with a bowl of soup or a nice green salad!

Preheat oven to Gas Mark 6 / 200°C / 400°F
And prepare muffin pan or use paper liners

In a large bowl add and combine with a fork or wire whisk

12oz / 350g	plain flour
1 Tablespoon / 15ml	baking powder
½ teaspoon / 2.5ml	salt
½ teaspoon / 2.5ml	coarse ground mixed pepper corns or black pepper
½ teaspoon / 2.5ml	bicarbonate soda
2oz / 60g	fine chopped walnuts

Variation: Instead of Boursin use Blue Cheese!

In a medium bowl add and combine with a wire whisk

2	large eggs, lightly beaten
4fl oz / 120ml	milk
4fl oz / 120ml	soured cream or plain natural yogurt
5oz / 150g	Boursin Cheese (150g package)
3oz / 85g	butter, melted
3 Tablespoons / 45ml	Scallions, finely chopped

TOPPING: 1oz / 25g chopped walnuts

Gradually fold wet ingredients into dry ingredients. Fold in with a large spoon or rubber spatula until combined, do not over-mix.

Spoon batter into 10 / 11 of the prepared muffin cups, fill to the top of each cup this will give a nice full sized muffin. Fill remaining cups half full with water to avoid burning the muffin pan and to give muffins moisture while baking.

Sprinkle tops with chopped walnuts 1oz / 25g will do, bake for 20 to 25 minutes or until tops spring back when gently touched. DO NOT OVER BAKE.   Allow to stand for one or two minutes, turn out on wire rack to cool.